WHY LEADERSHIP SUCKS
VOLUME TWO

Visit Miles online at www.milesanthonysmith.com and follow him on Twitter @Miles_Anthony.

Why Leadership Sucks: Volume Two: Senior Servant Leadership Fundamentals and the Pain, Pitfalls and Challenges

Cover Design: Books Go Social. booksgosocial.com

Cover Photo: Woman With Pacifier Image Used With Permission © Jason Stitt

Edited by Joy Tibbs (joyofediting.co.uk)

EPUB ISBN 978-0-9884053-8-7, Kindle ISBN 978-0-9884053-9-4; CreateSpace print ISBN: 978-0-9884053-7-0

Contents

Acknowledgments... *vii*

Introduction... *ix*

Part 1: To Serve or Not to Serve, That Is the
Question 1

1: Rejection and Hazards Call for Levity 3

2: Out of Touch?...7

3: Effective Leader or Abuser of
Accountability?...13

4: The Ubiquity of Greed and Dearth of Radical
Generosity 21

5: Does Emotional Sensitivity Help or
Hinder?...27

6: When Should I Assume the Defenseless
Position? 31

7: Wrap-up: Find Your Underrated, Memorable
Identity 35

Part 2: 'Leggo' My Ego 37

8: Workaholism, Discontentment,
and Scholé..39

9: Momentum and Innovation 45

10: 'Can Kicking' and Ticking Time Bombs 51

11: Failure Preferred: That's What Feedback Is For 59

12: Delegation Disorder and Title Envy 65

13: Wrap-up: Feeling Uncomfortable Yet? 69

Part 3: The Danger of 'Persona Non Grata' 71

14: Courteous Communication 73

15: Pragmatic and Vulnerable, Not Idealistic and Guarded Negotiation 79

16: Asynchronous Communication in the Digital Age 85

17: Anything You Can Do, I Can Do Better? 89

18: Avoid an Assumption-Fueled, Bigger Mess of a Mistake 97

19: Wrap-up: Appropriate Relationship Separation 103

Part 4: Fierce Competition Steamrolls Ahead 107

20: Constant Flux Demands Pig-Pen Leadership 109

21: Babies Don't Always Grow Up to Be Businessmen 113

22: Reject the Myths of the Masses... Starting with PI 119

23: Manage My Boss? Seize Responsibility and Autonomy? 129

24: Digital Marketing Mashup 133

25: Ignore Money and Board Issues at Your Own Peril 137

26: Closing Thoughts: Don't Be a NAG 145

My Current and Forthcoming Books and Resources *147*

Other Leadership Books I Recommend *154*

About the Author *155*

Acknowledgments

While there are many who have influenced my thinking on leadership, a number of whom I reference in this book, there are several people who challenged me to write and publish it.

The writings of Seth Godin encouraged me to 'poke the box' and to 'ship' this and other books. Seth, you may never know the depth of inspiration and motivation that got me started on this author journey.

Thank you to Google Drive and ListNote (khymaera.com), whose cloud storage and voice-to-text apps helped me compile notes, manuscripts, and images.

Thank you to Scott Gilbert, a lawyer, David Yeghiaian at Holy Family Memorial, Terry Kohler at Vollrath, and Jerry Baumann at Windway Capital for inspiring me to be a better servant leader.

Thank you to Michelle Smith at Violets are Blue Photography for the incredible photos you took for this book.

Thank you to the team at Books Go Social (booksgosocial.com) for the cover art. If you need any graphic or website design, please contact them via their website.

Thank you to my lovely wife Carolyn, who challenges me, holds me accountable, and loves me for who I am, not what I do. To my three children, Josiah, Reagan, and Dominic, thank you allowing me to be a child at heart.

Thank you to my editor, Joy Tibbs! You were an extraordinary help in so many ways. I could not have polished this book without your invaluable effort. If you are looking for an editor, reach out to her via her website (joyofediting.co.uk).

Thank you to everyone else with whom I have had the privilege to cross paths. You have all impacted my life in some way that has contributed to this work.

And last but not least, thank you to Christ, without whom I am nothing, even on my best day.

Introduction

In this day and age, we talk about leadership and more and more books are available on the subject than ever before. Yes, I know I'm adding to that pile.

The single keyword 'leadership' offers up more than 640 million search results on Google alone, and via the internet we can access leadership courses (like mine on Udemy.com) and online information more quickly and easily than ever before. We have more management consultants than ever before in the history of the world. Yet we have a severe lack of leadership in most areas of government, business, and even non-profit organizations.

So why is that? I believe it is a lack of follow-through... plain and simple. We all gorge ourselves on leadership conferences, webinars, books, and so on, but how much do we actually put into practice?

This book is about putting what we learn into practice, and it is a hallmark of the servant leadership and Level 5 leadership style that I try to emulate every day. I work hard to do what I say I am going to do and follow through on it. This puts some of us ahead of the pack, and I would invite you to join those ranks.

It really boils down to leadership fundamentals. Whenever we feel frustrated or life seems to be spinning out of control, we need to get back to the fundamentals; to the basics of why we're living. What is your purpose and mission? Is it based on the fundamentals of living a selfless life as a service-minded person?

> "Life and people aren't out to get you, but your approach to life and approach to people are."

At times when our lives feel out of control, we need to get back to the basics of life and leadership. We can get so distracted by things in life that we forget about what is seminally true. It is always about the fundamentals: fundamentals in work, life, sports, faith, and relationships. We can easily allow ourselves to become distracted by all kinds of things that really don't matter, and most of the time a return to the fundamentals brings us back into balance and promotes peace in our lives.

That's what this book is about. If you feel that things are out of control, either in your own leadership or in that of others around you, this book is for you. If you just want to learn more about servant leadership fundamentals, this book is also for you. It is my hope and belief that this book will help you get back to the fundamentals of life and leadership. These are the things that really matter in life, and life should not be focused on the things that distract us from the purpose of living a selfless life.

So what is servant leadership? Simply put, it combines a personal humility with a fierce resolve, and it is based on the teachings of Christ. Robert K. Greenleaf coined the term in 1970, but the concept began more than 2,000 years ago with the teachings of Christ.

In *The Power of Servant-leadership,* Greenleaf wrote: "The servant-leader *is* servant first… It begins with the natural feeling that one wants to serve, to serve *first.* Then conscious choice brings one to aspire to lead. That person is sharply different from one who is *leader* first, perhaps because of the need to assuage an unusual power drive or to acquire material possessions… The leader-first and the servant-first are two extreme types.

Between them there are shadings and blends that are part of the infinite variety of human nature."

Can we achieve servant leadership without the teachings of Christ? Not really. I am amazed at how many people don't realize that the term 'servant leadership' comes from His teachings. I have often heard people complain that my first book, *Why Leadership Sucks Volume 1,* uses too many Bible verses relating to Jesus, even though He started the whole servant leadership movement.

Some erroneously think that the whole concept is a recent phenomenon. It seems ironic to me that some people who are strong proponents of servant leadership don't understand that connection. You really can't have one without the other. You can't just be a do-gooder as a servant leader without acknowledging the teachings of Jesus Christ.

I've had people ask me, "Why do you talk about Jesus and the Bible in your leadership book, or in any business book for that matter?" My leadership book is called *Why Leadership Sucks* because Christ is at the center of servant leadership, and He experienced many rejections, which culminated in his crucifixion. Leading others in following His example invites similar frustrations and rejections to those that He experienced, except for the death part. Choosing to lead as Christ did is hard, since we don't get to pass the buck. Jesus' teachings are recorded in the Bible. He was a real, historical person. You may deny that He was the Son of God, but He really lived, and that's no debatable matter.

It seems kind of ironic that people would follow servant leadership without realizing they are following many of Christ's teachings. Some people have a problem with quoting Christ's sayings, but make no mistake; they are part and parcel of the servant leadership philosophy. His teachings are true, and there are tangible benefits if you follow His life instructions.

Even if you are not a devout Christian but you lead a life according to His servant leadership principles, you will see the benefits. However, the best benefits come from believing and following Him, recognizing that the only way for us to be our best is through Him, not by ourselves. Make no mistake; if you follow the truths in the Bible without believing its truth you will experience blessing during your lifetime, but not for eternity.

You may feel you have an idea of what servant leadership is by now, but perhaps you are wondering what Level 5 leadership is.

This concept was first introduced by Jim Collins, author of world-renowned business book *Good to Great*. Conveniently, Level 5 leadership dovetails with servant leadership.

Jim identified five levels that leaders can potentially attain. Some are able to get to level 5, while others get stuck at one of the lower levels.

Level 1 is a highly capable individual. This person gains success through his or her own hard work, skills, and determination.

Level 2 is a contributing team member. At this stage, he or she has found out how to be an effective team member by leveraging others' work in addition to their own.

Level 3 is a competent manager: a leader who organizes a team of people and financial resources to reach a particular goal or milestone.

Level 4 is an effective leader: a person who is able to cast a clear and compelling vision, and to marshal a team to achieve a high performance level in aiming for that vision.

Level 5 is the highest level. Leaders at this stage are able to build enduring greatness (over many years or even decades) through a paradoxical combination of personal humility and professional resolve.

LEVEL 5 LEVEL 5 EXECUTIVE
Builds enduring greatness
through a paradoxical combination
of personal humility plus professional will.

LEVEL 4 EFFECTIVE LEADER
Catalyzes commitment to and vigorous pursuit
of a clear and compelling vision; stimulates
the group to high performance standards.

LEVEL 3 COMPETENT MANAGER
Organizes people and resources toward the effective
and efficient pursuit of predetermined objectives.

LEVEL 2 CONTRIBUTING TEAM MEMBER
Contributes to the achievement of group
objectives; works effectively with others in a group setting.

LEVEL 1 HIGHLY CAPABLE INDIVIDUAL
Makes productive contributions through talent, knowledge,
skills, and good work habits.

HARVARD BUSINESS REVIEW

So why does leadership suck? It sucks because you get calls at the weekend and on your vacation days. It's harder to take a sick day because work piles up on the leader's desk that cannot be delegated or delayed. You have to take time out of your day and your own tasks to deal with team members who are not getting along or to listen to them complain about something they don't like. Then you either have to stay late to get your own work done or take it home with you.

You have to deal with more of the organizational politics the higher up the chain of command you are, which adds more work and complexity to the decisions you make. Your decisions will always leave some or most people unhappy. You have to constantly keep your boss or board of directors happy with your performance, in addition to those reporting to you. So not only are you managing those who are hierarchically below you; you also have to manage the expectations and perceptions of those above you.

This book is volume two of the *Why Leadership Sucks* series. If you haven't read volume one you don't *have* to do so before you read volume two. However, I do recommend reading volume one as it provides junior leadership lessons, words of wisdom, and powerful experiences that aren't included in volume two. Added to this, volume two contains lessons that build on those in volume one.

The leadership lessons in volume two are divided into four sections. In part one I deal broadly with the topic of service, exploring the choices we make in terms of whether to serve or not to serve. Part two focuses on setting aside your ego to do what's best for the team. Part three focuses on humility by avoiding persona non grata (being an unwelcome person). Finally, part four applies these concepts to the organizational world: demonstrating how to get results in specific situations, despite fierce marketplace competition.

To thank you for purchasing the paperback or ebook version of *Why Leadership Sucks Volume Two*, I am giving you my audiobook on a completely complimentary basis! Whoa, wait a cotton-pickin' minute! "Did I hear you right, Miles?" Yes, you did. All I ask in exchange is that you provide your email address... the one you regularly use (not your generic signup email addy). Hey, I spend a ton of my own time and money recording, editing, mastering, and publishing my audiobook on Audible, iTunes, and Amazon, so it's only fair for you to supply me with a real email address, and I'm happy to provide you with the complimentary audiobook in exchange. And it's not an abridged version; it's the entire audiobook.

To get it, go to

milesanthonysmith.com/wls2audiobook

and use password

GIMMEMYWLS2AUDIOBOOK

Go check it out right now. I'll wait for you to come back to the book! You may want the audiobook version to listen to the contents for the first time or to listen again as a refresher later while you're driving, working out, cooking, washing dishes, buying groceries, shoveling snow, mowing the lawn, eating lunch, doing data entry, waiting at a doctor's office, getting a massage, fishing, painting, or wrapping presents... I think you get the idea that an audiobook can be enjoyed while multitasking; something you can't do with a physical book or ebook!

WARNING!

Many of these concepts are true in the vast majority of cases, but there will always be minor exceptions. As is the case with any writing on the subject of leadership, there are so many variables (for-profit versus non-profit, politics, culture, small versus large organizations, etc.), not the least of which is human psychology, which can slightly or greatly alter the leadership prescription needed to solve your particular situation. So if you find yourself in a situation that might be an exception to the rule, please keep this in mind.

Part 1: To Serve or Not to Serve, That Is the Question

"The goal of leadership is not to be likable or loved, but to be proven trustworthy and respected."

There's a difference between liking someone who is in authority and respecting them. You don't have to love or even like someone to respect them, but you do have to gain their respect if you want to continue working for them long term. That is, if you want to enjoy your job. As leaders, our goal should be to earn the respect of those who report to us, not simply because of our positional authority but because of our own earned trust and authority.

Many who are just starting out in leadership wrongly think: "Now that I'm in charge, these 'peons' have to respect me!" And then we are rudely awakened to the fact that while we have positional authority that can coerce or force people to do a task, the better way is to earn the team's respect. Doing the latter will cause most people to want to follow you, leading to much greater productivity and loyalty throughout the process.

Comfort, control, and significance. I must attribute these three motivations to a discussion I had with Andy Kilgas, a good friend of mine. Thanks Andy! We all pay homage to one or more of these 'gods'. Which one is most important to you? Stop and think about it for a few minutes. Do you make decisions based on what is comforting to you? Or based on how you can control people, money, and situations to your personal advantage? How do you influence rather than coercing others to gain genuine significance in their eyes through trust and integrity?

It is important to recognize which one(s) we fall hard for and reduce their negative influences in our lives. It might be one or all three. Which do you struggle with the most? Take a minute to ponder on this and find ways to guard against it ruling your life.

1

Rejection and Hazards Call for Levity

"Crap should run uphill, not downhill."

Nevertheless, this is the opposite of what so often happens in real life. It would be nice if the boss sometimes had to deal with the problems that normally flow downhill. If so, perhaps he or she wouldn't be so quick to dismiss a timely warning, or would take more time to understand the nuance of the situation, or would plan more effectively rather than blindly forging headlong into a project.

These thoughts swarm around in our heads when it comes to our bosses, but how often do we take the time to self-assess whether we are doing the exact same thing to our own teams? This is the essence of servant leadership. It is a choice to serve the best interests of the team, sacrificing our own interests in the process.

"Leadership is often hazardous to your health."

When you experience rejection as a leader, it usually occurs for one of three reasons:

Hey, you suck at this leadership thing. If this is true, it requires humility to see it and focus on practicing servant leadership skills that lead to wisdom.

You are not sending out the right messages. Perhaps you're not communicating the way that a particular person wants to hear it or in a way that they can understand. This stems from a desire for others to be more like ourselves instead of recognizing that we, as leaders, need to talk in a way that suits them more than us. It is very difficult to do this well.

There is something wrong that is outside of your control, and you're just really not the right fit for that particular role.

If you do experience rejection in leadership, recognize that it might be number three. Maybe your leadership isn't the right fit or the timing is off. But don't skip to number three without honestly considering the first two reasons. We all have blind spots where there is room for improvement.

Our weaknesses as workers are amplified when we become leaders. If you seek revenue growth when your company is struggling, you might want to focus on your leadership tactics before going after growth, because it could crush you. I've seen many companies celebrate when fast growth happens and others that pursue it at all costs. Some companies aren't prepared to handle the operational aspects of their business as their customer orders explode. Think about the additional shipping, customer service, manufacturing, etc.

Others get drunk with success and start pursuing ancillary investments that don't have much to do with their core brand and end up alienating their customer base or running marginally profitable segments of their business that end up diverting time and investment away from other more profitable areas. Others simply underestimate the cash needed during growth, including major investments in inventory, staffing, and equipment that far exceeds the cash flow returns from those growth activities.

Often we run from the things we don't want to face. Perhaps our 'shiny object' focus is the result of avoiding leadership shortcomings in ourselves or within the team. This doesn't mean that we can't go after something new if it makes strategic sense for the organization, but we should be cautious, honest, and self-aware enough to ask ourselves what our motivation for change is.

Some people have a seemingly insatiable desire to be in charge. These people are very different from those who don't feel a burning need to be in charge but instead choose to be in leadership at the right times. The latter can easily step in and out of leadership roles without always having to lead. This doesn't mean they don't have the desire and natural gifting to lead others, but they don't seek it at all costs. The former is afraid of losing his or her position of power and will do anything to retain it, even at the expense of others.

So ask yourself if you have an unnatural desire to lead in every circumstance or if you can step back and let others lead at times. First you lead, then another leads, producing a graceful leadership dance.

"When in hazardous situations, don't brake and turn the wheel."

Just like when you're driving a car in snow, ice, or heavy rain, you want to avoid braking and turning at the same time. Do one or the other as an isolated action or complete them sequentially. If you try to do both, you may spin your car, or organization, out of control, especially during a crisis. Sometimes, the harder you work to try to make something happen, the more it slips through your fingers like sand. You need to make sure that your work isn't perceived to be an act of desperation.

"Balance humor with a focus on getting things done."

We all have a tough job as leaders; it isn't easy. And because of the pressures and stress, we often focus on the task at hand, urging our teams onward and upward while forgetting to enjoy the experience along the way.

Find a way to laugh with your team. This will do wonders to lift each other's spirits, especially during challenging times. Try dissipating a tense situation with an appropriate joke. Be mindful, however, when it comes to joking about sensitive topics such as an increase or decrease in staff salaries, or the dreaded lay-offs. Remember that what might seem funny to us at the time may not be so funny to others. If someone has just died, for example, a joke would not be appropriate, but there are many ways to poke fun at ourselves as leaders when things aren't going well.

One of my jokes around the office is that: "*I'm* the director, and it's all *my* fault." This is tongue-in-cheek, but it's true that, as leaders, the buck stops at our desks. The way I joke with my team is the result of trust that has been built over time and it won't necessarily work the same way for you. So find a way to inject humor that fits your situation; it's critical to your team's sanity. When you are able to help ease your team's stress levels they will be reinvigorated and ready to help you achieve much greater things than they would if they were still feeling frustrated.

2

Out of Touch?

"If you get overtaken by a semi-trailer truck on
a two-lane highway, you're going too slow."

I have literally witnessed the above, which was shocking
at the time, since there was a significant risk that the
semi wouldn't be able to pass the other car before an
approaching vehicle appeared in the oncoming lane.

This is a simple yet powerful illustration of what can
happen in leadership. Either we have team members (the
car) who are going too slowly, while the leader (the
semi) is forced to pass them (leave them behind) because
they aren't keeping pace any more, or the opposite can
happen, where the leader passes the entire team and is
so far ahead that others cannot keep up, no matter how
hard they try. To help with leadership pacing, collect
your thoughts and give them time to 'marinate' before
you blurt them out to your team.

Likewise, you can go too slowly and miss opportunities to move a project forward more efficiently. Sometimes a project needs to be set aside so resources can
be allocated elsewhere. When discussing potential new
projects, you may have heard someone say, "Why can't
we just try it and see if it works?" Now, there is a danger
in taking resources from one area and putting them into
another because we all have a limit to our resources,
even if you work for a company that turns over $100

million a year or more, but on occasion this is the most sensible option.

Sometimes it is more of a danger to try something because of what you must choose to stop doing in place of the new idea. If the existing project is important, there is an opportunity cost that needs to be taken into account. Don't forget to count the opportunity cost before giving anything up in favor of a new project.

Being out of touch or being perceived to be out of touch is very dangerous in a senior leadership role. When this happens, trust is broken and confidence in your ability to lead is lost. This happened to me once, earlier in my career, and it ended badly with me only staying with the organization for a few months.

My boss had begun to suspect that I didn't know what was going on with my team, which was partially true. I had signed on to work with a struggling company; so much so that I had to hire fifteen people in ninety days for a company of forty or so people. I even lost the HR manager, who was helping me hire and onboard all these new people. Needless to say, I was in a tough spot. I had to spend so much time hiring that I spent less time focusing on the day-to-day operations than I should have.

Given the massive turnover margin, it would have taken more than a few months to turn the ship around, but I didn't survive long enough to accomplish that. When the new senior leader came in, he or she didn't have to deal with the high level of turnover from day one.

This is a cautionary tale, which demonstrates that, even in tough situations, we can't afford to become out of touch or to give others the impression that we are out of touch. My boss believed it was the former and I the latter, but either way I had based my trust on my front line manager's ability to manage the day-to-day operations while I focused intently on replacing many team members, and this created the wrong impression.

"You will *always* underestimate subordinates' efforts."

Be careful when you judge somebody with regards to the job they're doing. We have the responsibility and right to judge people who work for us, and we have to keep them accountable by overseeing their work in order to determine whether they are measuring up to the expectations of the job.

However, we often fail to understand all the duties and responsibilities they have because we don't see them on a daily basis. So we should guard against underestimating the value each individual brings to our team. If we base our opinions of their work simply on what they tell you during your weekly update meetings with them, we will be glossing over a ton. There is likely to be much more going on beneath the surface, and it's usually more than you want to know, so trust them more.

With each degree of separation (level of hierarchy) you are from senior management, it becomes easier to criticize their decisions because you don't know what they know. You're out of touch with what's going on, and as you move up the career ladder and get closer to that information, your understanding grows. Then you know what's really going on and what your leaders are dealing with, and your view of management changes. You see how hard it is and that the decisions made are usually based on what's best for the entire team or company; not on what will make one person happy.

It's like living in a major city, Boston for instance. For every layer of management on top of your position you add distance between yourself and another major city in the United States: first Washington DC, then Charlotte, Atlanta, Nashville, Chicago, Minneapolis, Dallas, Denver, and so on. This can go on indefinitely, depending on how many layers your organization's management structure has.

The more we travel literally (to other states and countries) and figuratively (up the leadership ladder), the more our eyes are opened to new worlds we didn't know existed. Each time we are in a better position to understand what our past bosses knew. However, the danger is that we often start to forget what it was like on the front lines. We should recognize that, as leaders, we're always going to underestimate the amount of effort, time, and money that will be required of others to complete a project or task we have requested of them.

The reason for this is that the further away you are from project or task – meaning that you don't have to do it with your own hands, time, or resources – the more your memory of what it was actually like fades without you even realizing it. And the further away we are from that work and the more time that has lapsed since we did it, the harder and harder it becomes to accurately gauge how long a task should take or how easily it can be accomplished.

This is a huge problem in leadership, in that the further away we get from front line action, the more likely we are to have unrealistic expectations. This is something we must all be mindful and cautious of in order to guard against this potential blind spot when we find ourselves in charge.

"But I'm a vision guy/gal."

There is a distinct difference between fantasy and vision, but many leaders use vision as an excuse for a lack of proper planning and preparation. This leads to poor execution and burnout among your team because everything is last minute (instead of just a few things, which is always unavoidable). Don't fall for the lie that if we, as leaders, simply cast our vision and plunge headlong into it, things will take care of themselves.

Likewise, don't believe that other people can keep pace with your vision for the future. There is likely to be a tension here, since leaders need to keep pushing things forward, just not at breakneck speed. Also avoid the habit of trotting things out before they are a sure thing and are ready to be followed through. If you discuss ideas that you're not ready to implement quite yet, hold your enthusiasm or you will routinely disappoint with the perception that you don't deliver on your promises.

Patience is a virtue of leadership. If you don't get this right you will become the boy (leader) who cried wolf. You will lose the trust of people beneath you, and then when you legitimately cry wolf they will ignore your clarion call.

3

Effective Leader or Abuser of Accountability?

"There is a fine line between overbearing accountability and allowance for mistakes."

As leaders, we know that we need to hold people accountable for getting things done on time and in the right way, but the line is often blurred. How do we set reasonable, yet stretching expectations for others while avoiding micromanagement? We should hold people accountable for what is within their control but not what is outside it.

The line between accountability and 'not my fault' or 'out of my control' is a very fine one, and I've worked for bosses who play both sides of the fence. I also struggle with this concept, but if we regularly battle with it at least we are acutely aware of the issue. We don't want to enable 'excuse makers' here, but if people feel threatened by our micromanagement they won't do their best work. They will do just enough to get by.

Positive reward always outperforms a negative consequence in the long run. Tell someone that if they accomplish 'X' goal, you will give them a $500 bonus and you will have an engaged, motivated team member. Yell at the same person, "I'm taking this mistake out of your paycheck" and you will have broken trust with and demotivated that person. You may say that you don't care and that it is the employee's job to get their work done, no matter how he or she is treated. This would be an idealistic way of looking at things. It simply doesn't work that way, especially with younger generations entering the workforce, who are allergic to the "Do what I say because I'm in charge" mentality. They want to be inspired to follow a leader rather than being dictated to.

It's possible to be in touch in some ways and out of touch in others, not even realizing you are micromanaging your team. That's what is so dangerous because it's hardest to spot your own micromanagement. You may think you're focusing on the right things when you are in fact micromanaging the situation. You may be in touch with what's going on each day, but you may be out of touch with the more strategic, bigger-picture issues that are more important than the details. If we aren't careful, we may genuinely think we're in touch when we're really out of touch with the core strategy.

"So what do we do to avoid this blindness, Miles?" I hear you ask, and I'm glad you did. The key is to surround yourself with trustworthy people and give them explicit permission to point this out. Let them know that you won't be upset and that you expect them to give you unvarnished feedback. Then don't be upset when it happens and thank them for increasing your effectiveness by drawing attention to any blind spots.

We also need to be careful not to be 'pigeonholers'. If you give people the opportunity to grow, you'll be amazed at what they can learn and adapt, while the opposite is true if you pigeonhole to the point where you are constraining their personal or professional growth. This happens when we allow certain mental pictures to remain so firm in our minds that we hold people to a certain spot, personality type, job, or skillset. Had we opened our minds to the possibility that they could change, we might have afforded them a grand opportunity.

When we place people in boxes, we overestimate our ability to read and know what's best for them. Now, I'm not saying that we can't learn to read people, but I am suggesting that we need to be cautious not to think of ourselves so highly that our thoughts become self-fulfilling prophecies, dooming others to only being good at 'X' and not 'Y' or 'Z'. I know I don't want to be the type of leader who holds other people back from fulfilling their potential and destiny.

> "There's a difference between a leader who settles for a poor performer and one who chooses to lay down his selfish ambition and pride to coach and mentor someone."

Our tendency as leaders is to fall into one or more of the following groups:

1. Detail manager
2. Coach
3. Delegator

Most of us recognize these terms and know what the normal state of each should be, so let's talk about the extremes. Firstly, following up on things that matter is important, but detail managers, at their most extreme, want to control every little detail, no matter how puny.

Detail managers can spend too long listening to every personal issue their staff members have, leaving little time to get work done. Having said this, we all want bosses who will take us under their wing and mentor us a bit. That's healthy, and that's what a good coach-style manager will do.

Detail Manager

Effective Leader

Coach

Delegator

Finally, hyper-delegators do zero work themselves, yet expect it all to be done by the following day. Leaders do need to delegate to others to expand the capacity of what can be done, but delegating everything is unfair and counterproductive.

The intersection of these three constructs is where an effective leader stands. Aim for as much of a balance between them as possible.

"If you always do what you've always done,
you'll always get what you've always got"
(Henry Ford, founder of the Ford Motor
Company).

The reason most organizations never grow, or stop growing at a certain point, comes down to the limitations of the leader or leadership team. They want to control and micromanage the organization, but in order to promote growth it cannot be micromanaged or controlled. There is often a fear of loss of control as the company gets larger. I'm not suggesting there shouldn't be any checks or balances or accountability, but a hands-off approach is required in some areas if the organization is to grow.

As leaders, we have to keep growing in order for our organizations to do the same. Many leaders and managers tend to look at salaried employees' (those exempt from overtime) wages in the same we do with the wages of hourly, non-exempt workers. We want to scrutinize the number of hours our salaried employees work when we should really be focusing on whether they are getting the job done and achieving results.

They may be completing their work with excellence, and, if so, it doesn't really matter how many hours they work because they're performing well. Maybe you want to give them more work, which is certainly your right as a leader. However, if salary-exempt employees are underperforming and failing to put in the hours, a discussion needs to be had about improving their performance and getting the job done. There should be a clear distinction between these two types of employee.

Many of us also have hourly (non-exempt) workers. When it comes to these, don't forget to be aware of the switch that needs to happen when things go from being terribly busy to when the workload becomes lighter. The worst thing you can do as a manager is to ignore this, since most people will slack off and the work will be divided inefficiently among staff, with those who have more tasks resenting the others who have fewer.

Part of a manager's job is to continually spread out the work among the team. There is nothing worse than a person who is being paid on an hourly basis just waltzing through their day. Plus, when the work picks up again, those with a previously lighter load will resent the normal, faster pace.

"Micromanagement is the destroyer of momentum."

There are basically two extremes when it comes to the types of people you will manage: those who are unmotivated, and those who are self-motivated, some of whom are easily discouraged. There are shadings between these extremes, to be sure. You will have to motivate the former each and every day as they have little, if any, self-motivation. You won't need to motivate the latter, but you will need to encourage them. Because they have strong self-motivation they will work so hard that sometimes they can feel discouraged. They have sky-high expectations of themselves and often can't see the forest for the trees in what they have already achieved. They are working extremely hard and always striving to make something happen, but encourage them to regularly take a step back from the day-to-day grind and reflect on all that has been accomplished.

On the other hand, be careful about giving too much encouragement to those who are not self-motivated because they will become full of themselves and think they're doing a great job when they actually need a bit more motivation to get their work done. This usually involves setting clear deadlines for each task, not just the main projects, which can become time-consuming and draining. This doesn't mean that you can't give them *some* encouragement, just focus more on encouraging those who regularly become discouraged, despite their great efforts.

4

The Ubiquity of Greed and Dearth of Radical Generosity

"It is not a matter of whether there is greed in our leadership; it is a measure of the degree to which greed permeates our lives."

We all have areas in our lives where greed resides, but greed is hardest to spot in ourselves. We owe it to ourselves and to others to find that specific area and become intentionally generous in it in order to combat greed. Accepting the fact that we will likely always struggle in this area and making peace with that daily struggle will be key to winning the battle. The other key is in surrounding ourselves with people who will speak the truth in love about our greed.

Early in my career, I was contemplating firing a team member and, in the midst of that thought, found myself realizing that if I did, I, among others, would personally benefit from that person's forfeiture in our company's 401k retirement plan. Had I not been self-aware enough to recognize my shameful thought, I could have let this sway my decision to terminate this person's job.

The question is not whether we are greedy or generous, since most of us can find something generous about ourselves to trumpet while we hide, or are unaware of, other greedy behavior. It is simply about asking ourselves, "Where is the greed?" Even those of us who consider ourselves to be generous must be introspective if we really want to root it out.

I admit that it's hard to see my own greed, but the more I challenge myself to look into every area of my life – be it work, friends, family, or other relationships – I have had my eyes opened to pockets of greed tucked away in the recesses of my mind and thoughts. I challenge you (and myself) to look in various areas, and I bet we will all find something somewhere that reveals greed, even if it appears in a seemingly insignificant way.

It might even be in specific area in which ninety-five percent of the time we are being very generous and think we're doing well. Even if it's only five percent of the time or situational, meaning that we are generous with our money with everyone but our immediate family, for example, we need to challenge ourselves and shine a light on those areas in which we are not generous, then work to combat this with intentional generosity.

And don't think that this only applies to your personal life. Greed also matters at work. If you allow greed to direct your leadership, your team will suffer and your organization will limp along under that weakness until you confront and deal with it.

"Choosing generosity is *always* good for business... in the long term."

You may be saying to yourself, "What does generosity have to do with this leadership thing?" It has everything to do with it. Our world is dying for other people's generosity as we are experiencing a dearth of it. It is a natural law that, when we are generous, blessings come back to us and our organizations. These blessings aren't always financial; it could be better business relationships, improved health or fewer team problems, for example.

More importantly, giving to receive blessings isn't the point. Giving demonstrates that we recognize we can't do whatever we are doing without others. We can't hoard enough of our time, money, or resources to be successful in the long term. If you talk to people who have been successful over an entire lifetime, you will hear over and over that they chose to be routinely generous.

Now, you will want to hide some of this generosity, but sometimes you may want others to 'catch you in the act' in order to inspire them to similar feats. International marriage expert Mark Gungor, whom I used to work for, once relayed a story to me about his father's funeral. Everyone who showed up at the funeral gushed about all the many wonderful things Mark's father had done for them. Most of these things Mark never seen or heard about, which was simultaneously heartening and disheartening to Mark. Nobody had ever told Mark about these good deeds, and had his dad shared some of them, how much more of an impact might that have had on Mark's ability to grow into generosity as a child, young adult, and mature adult? If we never see generosity displayed, we may find it hard to be generous ourselves as we assume that it doesn't matter.

When I was in high school at Booker T. Washington in Tulsa, OK, I participated in a student exchange program to Germany. I grew up in a home that followed the teachings of Christ and attended weekly church services. My parents showed me that the teachings of Christ instructed us to give ten percent of our income to a local church. So when I visited a Catholic church in Germany with my exchange family, I naturally put DM50 (about $30) into the offering plate. My exchange mate was shocked and almost horrified that I would give that much money. She fiercely tried to stop me, but I gently and firmly insisted.

I didn't hide the generosity of my giving on this occasion, but another time I hid it from view. I was with my wife and our three children at the Tundra Lodge waterpark in Green Bay, WI, and when I went to buy food and drinks for my family there was a lady in front of me whose credit card had been declined. I couldn't tell exactly what the guy behind the counter had said to this lady, but I think he had told her she could come back and pay later. When I placed my order I told the guy I would pay for her order. She had already gone, so she didn't know. And I doubt she ever knew, even if she came back to pay later, since the guy at the counter would have said that someone had paid for her order but couldn't remember who it was. I never told my family as I chose to avoid the plaudits on that occasion.

Another time when I was at a restaurant, Cheddar's in Tulsa, OK, I noticed the waitress was having a particularly tough day. I left a $50 tip for a $10 meal, and although I tried to leave before she found out, she came back to the table crying and profusely thanking me, saying that I had made her day better, despite all the problems she was dealing with. There is no right or wrong way to hide or expose our generosity; just endeavor to do some of both.

"One gives freely, yet grows all the richer;
another withholds what he should give, and
only suffers want" (Proverbs 11:24, ESV).

If we are not equally comfortable giving *and* receiving kindness or generosity, we are equally selfish. I want to challenge you to be radically generous. So many of us, myself included, have a selfish streak inside us and don't want to give away what we have for free. So give away your book, give away your time, give away your money. Whatever you have that is of value, give it away.

Giving something hurts and it's good to feel that tinge of pain when you give sacrificially. It means that the selfish part of you is dying. We'll never completely rid ourselves of that selfish part; the pain is there to remind us to give rather than hoarding. The fear is that, in giving things away, we won't have enough to provide for ourselves and our families, but the truth is, the more we give away, the more we will receive both tangibly and intangibly, and ultimately it is what Christ's teachings call us to do.

So be radically generous in areas in which you recognize that you are somewhat greedy. And remember that greed is the hardest thing to see in ourselves, so ask someone who knows you well and is trustworthy for some perspective on the areas in your life that exhibit greed. The only antidote to greed is regularly practiced, radical, intentional generosity.

5

Does Emotional Sensitivity
Help or Hinder?

The answer to this question is that it depends...

I was watching Ken Burns' TV series, *The Civil War*, and was surprised to see that Ulysses S. Grant was both resolute in his ability to lead his troops into tough battle situations and showed a seemingly incongruous display of emotion (deep sorrow) when valuable leaders died in battle. Grant even broke down once and sobbed uncontrollably over the loss of one of his generals.

Many strong, courageous people throughout history have also had a very sensitive side and a good balance of both qualities. Periodic weeping is actually beneficial, in that it helps clear the soul and mind of negative emotions, pent-up frustrations and disappointments. Now, we shouldn't be crying all the time, which would demonstrate that we are constantly emotionally distraught, but at times it is good to hit that reset button.

Too often we view emotional sensitivity as a weakness, but it is quite the contrary. For leaders who know who they are, sensitivity is an incredible well of strength – that other, less secure leaders don't have – from which they can draw in tough times. The most dangerous leader is one who acts as though he is never sad, angry, or depressed, and constantly wears a fake masquerade mask.

All of us struggle with emotions, and those who make peace with them can be the most generous, gentle, calm, resolute, direct, honorable, and courageous people you will ever meet. That said, there are times when, as a leader, you don't have a choice when it comes to showing your emotions. You must act in the face of danger and keep them hidden. That doesn't mean you don't feel them; you simply choose to lead and act without hesitation or care for your own well-being. Knowing when to be authentic in allowing others to see your emotional sensitivity, as well as knowing when to set emotions aside, separates the mediocre leaders from the truly great ones.

So if you struggle in this area, cultivate your sensitive side. Don't be afraid to grieve any loss in business. You many leave an organization for another opportunity or experience someone else leaving. Perhaps a project is terminated, investor funding is cut off, your company goes bankrupt, you get transferred to a new department, or you get a new boss. We invest a ton of time and energy into these things, and it is okay to grieve the loss of them.

The tendency in business, in particular, is to become more cold and calculating, and less sensitive and less able to express our feelings as we move up the leadership ladder. We shouldn't be overly emotional, but we need to cultivate that sensitivity because being sensitive towards others will help us understand situations more clearly, which usually leads to a more informed and better decision.

If we take the time and develop the compassion to understand what's really going on, it will make our work world a better place rather than merely surviving in an unfeeling, uncaring, cold work environment. And don't forget that we may think our organizations are caring, but perception isn't always the reality. So if the majority of people view your organization as cold, you should take a long, hard look in the mirror and encourage your leaders to do the same.

"Be a radiator, not a carburetor."

Just as a radiator distributes coolant throughout the car, choose to radiate light, warmth, and positivity throughout your life. Don't suck all the life out of the people you are around, like a carburetor does. This is an easy analogy to remember, and it's both simple and true. People should be energized and uplifted by being around you; they shouldn't leave your presence feeling drained. I know this might seem trite, or sound as though we can never have a bad day when we feel depressed, but that's not what I'm saying. We just need to make sure we are being radiators more of the time than we are being carburetors.

6

When Should I Assume the Defenseless Position?

"Not my circus, not my monkeys" (Polish Proverb).

You must learn when to say, "That's not my job; it's not my responsibility" as well as knowing when to reject that notion. There is certainly a time and a place for both. Sometimes it's not our department's final call, and while you've genuinely tried to make a change your hands are tied. Ultimately, the other leader is responsible for that. By the same token, we shouldn't always say, "That's not my job so I'm not going to do anything about it", and not even try. That would amount to washing our hands of the problem. We should learn to recognize when we need to get involved and when we need to step back. There is a delicate balance between the two responses.

Be someone who draws in additional responsibility, not someone who does only the bare minimum or only what they're told, or solely what is specified in their job description. Because in the new economy, those who routinely go above and beyond will thrive and succeed in their current work and find it easier to get another job in the future. Learn how to draw in more responsibility than whatever was set down in your job description or in your boss' expectations, and in this way you will set yourself apart.

In the same way, strap on your flak jacket and take a few blame bullets. Choosing to take the metaphorical bullet for your team will build strong and fierce loyalty among those who you want on your team, and for those who don't, they won't care and it will be obvious that they're not the right fit for your team.

Don't assume responsibility for decisions you didn't make. Think about that for a minute. Let it sink in. Put yourself in a position where you have to let one of your team members go. If you haven't had to fire someone before, you may think you can't let so-and-so go because they are struggling financially or they just bought a new house or a new car. And while that may be true, and we genuinely want to be sensitive to others' situations, we can't assume responsibility for someone else's decisions.

We shouldn't make our decisions based upon the poor decisions of other people. We must make the best decision for the organization and recognize that sometimes other people will be (indirectly) negatively affected by our decision because of choices they or we have (directly) made, and that might make us uncomfortable. However, we cannot accept responsibility for their choices, only ours. Having said that, please don't use this as a way to make yourself feel better for the pain your decisions may cause. We all need to take responsibility for our actions.

There are other situations in which we need to assume the defenseless position and take the blame. A college buddy of mine and I went to Woodland Hills Mall in Tulsa, OK, and as I was pulling out of the parking lot I swiped a car in the adjacent parking space with my truck. I wasn't going fast and I wasn't distracted; I simply misjudged the distance between my truck and the car, which was damaged. My friend suggested we could leave without leaving my contact information on the owner's windshield.

I was tempted for a moment, but decided to do the right thing by leaving my information. I decided to pay for the collision repair out of my own pocket rather than filing an insurance claim, since my premiums would have gone through the roof. I was nineteen and male, so my premiums were already high, and I wanted to avoid them becoming astronomical. I had the car owner sign a release stating that, on receipt of my payment, he was releasing me from any and all liability. The car owner couldn't believe that I hadn't just driven away and was grateful that I had done the right thing.

We need to own up to these mistakes, no matter how painful or expensive they are, rather than trying to hide them. Either way, we will develop a habit of either owning up or hiding things. The former, while more painful in the short term, is better in the long term, as it will cause people to trust our leadership. The latter, while easier in the short term, has painful long-term consequences in terms of lost trust and lack of character, which can't be hidden forever.

Another reason leadership sucks is that we don't always get to defend ourselves because it requires more than just a simplified explanation or answer. For example, if we have to let an employee go, we can't go into the details to justify our position and validate the fact that letting that person go was mostly or even completely justified. It is tempting to try to explain very valid reasons for our decisions, but we can't always do it.

We may even be labeled and characterized by our teams as callous and heartless when the reality might be completely the opposite. That same person may have done many terrible things, unknown to their peers, but we cannot defend ourselves in certain these situations. So you will have to take the higher ground, which sucks, but a true leader does what is right, even when it is painful.

Be really careful about criticizing or being drawn into criticism of your predecessor. It is easy to get pulled into this trap. There might be some truth in what people who are frustrated with your predecessor are saying. Focus on the solution to the issues that weren't attended to beforehand and get those fixed first. Ignore the pull to get caught up in other people's venting about their frustrations with their previous supervisor. Believe me, they will tell you everything about what upset them, but be restrained.

7

Wrap-up: Find Your Underrated, Memorable Identity

"A man's gift makes room for him and brings him before the great" (Jewish proverb).

Our goal as leaders is to be underrated, always exceeding expectations, rather than the opposite, which is far too common among leaders today. This does not mean we should use this as an excuse to manipulate situations to our advantage by purposefully hiding our abilities, but it does mean that we shouldn't over-promote our skills and abilities. If we allow people to find out about them on their own rather than tooting our own horns too much, we will earn the respect of others as humble, trustworthy teammates who usually exceed expectations.

We also need to be memorable. I sold used cars for about two years early on in my career, and the top used car salesman was someone I looked up to. Robert Groom used to take a picture of the people in the car they had just purchased. Then he would put that image on the cover of a CD and create a soundtrack that the buyers got to choose. Then, every time they played the CD, they remembered Robert and referred other potential customers to him.

At the time, I thought it was a waste of time and money to take pictures, burn CDs, print labels, and assemble them, but I have now come to appreciate the value and memorability he was creating. Robert was always the number one or two used car salesperson during my tenure at Chris Nikel Chrysler Jeep Dodge in Tulsa, OK. We need our lives to be more like Robert's; more underrated, more memorable.

Part 2: 'Leggo' My Ego

"Tomorrow is a figment of your imagination; it doesn't really exist."

Far too often, we put ourselves and our own wants ahead of the needs of others in our personal lives, which is an empty way to live, but setting aside our own egos to do what's best for our organizations as leaders is even more important, for one simple reason. Leadership isn't about what is in our best interests, nor is it about what is solely in others' best interests. It simply comes down to what is best for all.

Now, we can take this to an extreme, with others' interests' masquerading as servant leadership, leading to us not taking care of ourselves. We may choose to skip physical exercise and social activities, or neglect family relationships all in a vain attempt to serve our organization's needs at all costs. At the other end of the spectrum, if we are single, without children and extended family or friends, we might be able to get by with a sole focus on ourselves, but in servant leadership within a business environment (as with family and friends), considering others' interests is critical. We have a responsibility that goes beyond ourselves, and we owe others our best leadership.

The leaders of our organizations, and especially the top leaders, such as presidents, CEOs, general managers, and executive directors, will have a natural bent toward a particular area based on their work experience. If they came from a finance or accounting background they're going to have more of a focus in that area. And if they didn't have a background in a particular area, for example marketing, they're not going to understand it as easily.

They will tend to undervalue the experience they don't have and overvalue their own. It's important to recognize how our own experiences guide us and how our lack of understanding can blind us in our leadership. These experiences can cause us, detrimentally, to lead in a way that puts our own interests first rather than the organization's needs.

8

Workaholism, Discontentment, and Scholé

"Never *completely* sacrifice yourself or your family's well-being or happiness on the altar of success. Period."

The key word here is 'completely'. On occasion, you will have to work a weekend, evening, or vacation as a leader, since work never takes a vacation. Just make sure it is truly necessary or this can become all-consuming if we enjoy our jobs and don't put up certain inviolable boundaries.

Wilmar Schaufeli, professor of work and organizational psychology at Utrecht University in the Netherlands, coined the phrase 'engaged workaholic'. He states that the crucial difference between a workaholic and one who is not a workaholic is the divide between those who feel pulled through the enjoyment of work and those who feel pushed by negative feelings, such as wanting to escape intimacy with a partner or family member.

The real danger with workaholism is that by working too many hours for too long, you will alienate your family and friends to such an extent that you will have no reason not to become even more of a workaholic. You will have no life outside work and no one to share it with. Short stints of more than forty hours per week are needed at times, so long as they are short-lived and don't drag on. If you are routinely working more than fifty hours a week, you either need to delegate more, or to stop doing unproductive or less important stuff. This starts with a prioritization of work and life responsibilities.

For me, the order of importance is: faith, family, work, education, and side hustle. Having this order clearly established in my head is extremely important for me, having learned from two workaholic parents. Early on in my career, I gave my wife permission to communicate to me when things were getting out of control.

There was a time when I worked as the general manager of a $2 million dollar company during the day, went to MBA classes two nights a week, did homework and studied in between, and still spent time with my wife and three children, the latter of whom were all born during my four-year MBA night school stint. Even now, I have a day job, family obligations (my oldest is a teenager now), and a side hustle in writing books and speaking at events.

"There is no such thing as work-life balance; what we need to establish is work-life tension."

Tension isn't always a bad thing. It helps us determine which aspect of our lives needs more attention at any given time. The statement "I work hard and play hard" is just an excuse to be a workaholic and a pleasure-a-holic. If you are seeking to overwork your body and overindulge in pleasure, you will burn out. Rest is needed. Things are always in a state of flux, so push the pedal on the bike that is up; the other one will come back

WHY LEADERSHIP SUCKS 2

around. If you alternate back and forth regularly, you won't have a major issue with work-life balance.

Take daily and quarterly breaks from work. This will provide mental diversion, which helps to reset things. Then, when you return to work you will be more productive. Find your scholé (the Greek word for 'leisure'). Even taking a ten or fifteen-minute break a couple of times a day could make you more productive than staying late, or perhaps you just need to do something restful in the evenings or at the weekend.

I like to unwind by spending time with my cat and riding my motorcycle, but not at the same time. Now, for all you cat haters out there, I was given a male Maine Coon cat for my first birthday. His name was Boots, and he lived until he was nineteen years old; as an outdoor cat, mind you. Since then, our family has had Butterscotch, a female cat who lived with us for fourteen years, and now Chase, a six-year-old, male, twenty-pound fat cat.

Speaking of scholé, there is something unique about riding a motorcycle: the wind in my hair (or lack of it, in my case), the open road, leaning side to side in turns, and the exhilaration of accelerating quickly melts away all of my stress. In addition to the weekly mental diversions, I need a several-day vacation away from the office every quarter. I start to get a little frustrated with things about once a quarter, and I have recognized the need to get away before I burn out. It does wonders.

Those of us in leadership roles, especially senior leadership roles, need to take a break from work every three to four months. There isn't really any magical reason behind this number; it's just what I have found helpful for me over the years. The reason leaders need to take regular time off is that the politics, people, and process issues that must be dealt with on a daily basis are mentally and emotionally taxing. Take at least two days off. If you can take a week off, it would be ideal to do so every quarter. This will give you an opportunity to be more introspective, which leads to greater innovation and creativity. When you are on the front lines of leadership you are simply exposed to more stress and more challenging situations than you otherwise would be.

"And which of you by being anxious can add a single hour to his span of life?"

(Matthew 6:27, ESV).

Far too often as leaders we feel the pressure of looming deadlines and the sheer volume of work that we are responsible for, and we allow that to convince us to skip lunch entirely or to eat lunch at our desks. I've done it and, frankly, I used to do it almost every day. But I found that I need to hit that reset button by not only leaving my office, but by sharing some time and a laugh or two with co-workers or friends.

While it's tempting to say that we can't afford to take a lunch break away from our desks, we need these mental breaks to be efficient in our work. And every time I choose to set aside that time, it is emotionally, mentally, and productively worth it. So get out of your office, eat with a co-worker or friend, go for a walk outdoors, or find another way to decompress, even if it's only for fifteen to thirty minutes. You will be refreshed and more efficient in your afternoon work if you do. And don't check your smartphone during your work break! Step away from the smartphone; everything will be okay! Allow yourself some time to properly relax.

We certainly should work hard, but we don't always need to try so hard to make things happen. Sometimes it's better to let them happen while you're working diligently rather than fretting over them. Otherwise you will wear yourself out, never realizing how crucial the timing of things is. If it's not the right timing, you will be banging your head against a brick wall.

"Mo Money Mo problems" (song title from The Notorious B.I.G.'s *Life After Death* album).

Will this situation that I'm so concerned about, consumed by, and frustrated with today matter in five years? This question can be used as a gauge to determine what really matters in life and to put those things into perspective. Continued frustration can lead to discontentment and to us buying the lie that the grass is greener on the other side of the fence. Sometimes it is, but very rarely. It is more likely that life is trying to show us something we need to work on.

It is very dangerous to measure our influence by the amount of money in our bank accounts. It may sound trite, but money isn't everything. And if we buy into this lie, it will lead us down a path of discontent. Discontentment is always followed by the temptation of distraction. Distraction can take many forms, including consumerism, addiction, and any type of selfish living. Don't fall for counterfeit distractions when servant leadership and selfless living, as Christ's life demonstrated, is the goal. Distraction is a cheap alternative to a fulfilling life of service to others.

"Do not toil to acquire wealth" (Proverbs 23:4, ESV).

Discontentment leading to distraction is born out of a longing for the paradise that existed before sin, suffering, pain, and death entered the world. The Garden of Eden in the Bible, which is no more, is the paradise we all long for. We are all part of the fallen human condition.

Any time we search for love or acceptance in the wrong ways, or are unhappy with our marriages, jobs, children, friends, money, cars or whatever else, this can drive our discontent. It reveals an underlying longing to get back to paradise and to be where things were perfect (God's way), without challenge and struggle. We live in a sinful, fallen world in which we must wrestle with that discontentment every day, but we must struggle well by refusing to allow it to control our lives.

Don't think that other departments or other organizations have it any easier than you do. It is a myth and a trap to believe otherwise. The truth is, things are just as challenging for others. Each department or organization has its own unique challenges. They aren't exactly the same, but we all have tough challenges, nonetheless. The same is true in our personal lives.

9

Momentum and Innovation

"A mind that is stretched by new experiences can never go back to its old dimensions" (Oliver Wendell Holmes, Jr., from *Autocrat of the Breakfast Table*).

I included a brief discussion about the perils of micromanagement earlier in this book, and now I want to explore the antagonist of the micromanager: the momentum creator.

World-renowned leadership expert Andy Stanley offers three simple keys to sustained momentum:

1. New

New triggers momentum, and everyone knows when the team has it. You can't fake it, no matter how hard you try. Anything new, by definition, generates some kind of momentum, which can either be positive or negative. Organizational momentum is often triggered by new leadership, new direction, or a new product or service. Momentum is never triggered by tweaking something old. It is triggered by introducing something new!

2. Improved

The new must be a significant improvement over the old if it is to have a positive impact. Ask yourself: "Is this a significant improvement over what we had before?" If you are in a situation where there isn't enough money to do something new and improved, you are doing too many things.

3. Improving

Momentum is sustained through continuous improvement. Continuous improvement requires regular, systematic, rigorous, unfiltered, and ongoing evaluation carried out by the people who helped create it.

You might be asking, "So how do I apply this new, improved, and improving strategy?" Start by evaluating your personnel, programming, season, product, service, look, and venues. Look for ways to dramatically upgrade what you do. Visit other successful organizations to see what they are doing. This will often spark innovative ideas.

> "The importance of momentum in your organization cannot be understated!"

Warning signs that you don't have momentum include: disengaged leaders, overactive management, complacency, complexity, or a breach or lack of trust. Trying to control, or worse, manipulate our teams will choke momentum, and since momentum is vital to the success of any team or organization, you will experience stagnation without it, which ultimately leads to the death of an organization, either slowly or quickly.

It is as difficult to start an organization, non-profit or for-profit, as it is to kill one. Starting or killing such an endeavor takes a lot of time and effort. In any new organization or startup, you are an entrepreneur if you are a leader. Once you have something in motion, it is very hard to destroy it. Organizations can be destroyed through bankruptcy or other means, but it is hard both to get one going and to stop that motion, even with poor management in the latter case.

It takes years to get a business, church or non-profit going, so expect it to take way longer than you think. While it used to take three to five years, now it is more like seven to ten. Then when you gain momentum, this momentum can seep out slowly, which is worse than an immediate crisis as many don't even realize they are losing it until it is too late.

So guard, protect, and build up momentum any way you possibly can; legally and ethically, of course. Protect it like you would a baby. It is the most precious commodity in any organization as it can make up for almost any organizational shortcoming, including poor leadership, inefficient people or processes, and overspending.

While it should be a goal to run our organizations in such a way that we avoid crisis by keeping things fresh and new, crisis does bring with it a great opportunity to break the status quo and change things that wouldn't otherwise be changed. Whether it is a crisis involving finances, employee turnover, safety of a product or something else, a moment of confusion or clarity may ensue.

It is often the responsibility of middle managers within the organization to take charge and take action to correct things that need to be changed, perhaps because the leaders at the top have been resistant to change before. During times of crisis, the executive leaders who were risk-averse suddenly become scared and more open to change. This offers a great opportunity for the right kind of change to take place, which will positively reposition the organization or department in a way that wouldn't be possible during a period of relative calm.

"There is a correlation between curiosity and creativity on the one hand, and innovation and successful leadership on the other."

This is true in business, even though we tend to elevate the logical, analytical side of what it takes to lead and manage an organization. On one hand, leading people and managing financial metrics requires more left-brain centered activity, and on the other, creativity and innovation is typically associated with right-brained activity. Yet in culture we elevate feelings above logic and reason.

People tend to say, "I feel this way or that", rather than, "I think" or "I believe". Our culture is shifting from reason and logic to something that is more feelings-based. While it may be more symbolic than anything, I challenge you to pay more attention every time you say, "I feel..." and consider whether to replace that with, "I think" or I believe". We tend to focus on the fact that most of us lean in one direction or the other. It is best to engage both sides, but remember that very few MBAs are artists, musicians, or other creative types.

Having both a strong analytical, results-oriented side and a sensitive, thoughtful, creative side is critical to winning in the workplace today. It is the synthetization of disparate ideas that is key to innovative and disruptive creation, and without this, companies will wither and die on the vine. We must continually innovate to avoid the commoditization of our products or services.

There are many examples of this, but one is the rise of grocery store branded products, which are competing with name brands on the very same shelf. If we don't continue to improve our products or services, they will become outdated, kind of like the buggy whip. For more detailed discussion on what drives creativity and innovation, check out *The Myths of Creativity: The Truth About How Innovative Companies and People Generate Great Ideas*, written by my friend David Burkus.

"Implement your creative and innovative ideas ASAP or someone else will."

Curiosity is a valuable leadership trait and is closely linked to creativity. Those who are more likely to wander off the path in seeking new information are the ones who usually spark something innovative. It shouldn't matter whether an innovative or creative idea came from the boss or another person on the front lines. No matter where the ideas come from, we need to approach them with equal parts caution and enthusiasm.

A good idea is a bad idea until it is properly vetted. New ideas that may sound good on the surface, especially to the person putting them forward, may not be so great when you get down to reality, practicality, and profitability. That may be a whole different story.

In our enthusiasm, we often run with what we initially think are really good ideas, but we don't always take the time to discern whether they are smart, risk-worthy business ideas. We cannot always discern which creative ideas will be successful or are actually bad ideas until we implement them. So at some point we have to finish the creative vetting process and ship that product or service. This separates the creative talkers from the doers. The doers will actually ship items and live with the consequences, good or bad. Talkers will get energized by talking but will be too afraid to actually do anything about their ideas. Be a doer; the world needs more of those.

When it comes to investing money into new ideas, we need to exercise extreme caution! I am a solid believer in bootstrapping innovation as much as possible as it lowers the risk of losing our investment money. Have a healthy fear when it comes to making investment risk a calculated risk. Don't be too afraid to take the risk, just make sure that you have a healthy respect for the money you're investing in a bid to grow a business that has the potential to bring in more money. People at the other end of the spectrum spend recklessly and don't really count the opportunity cost of the money they're investing.

10

'Can Kicking' and
Ticking Time Bombs

Make sure you have *all* the decision makers in the room when you are making decisions, especially key ones. You would think this should be common sense, but you might be surprised to hear how often this doesn't happen. We set up meetings to come to a conclusion on something but fail to ensure that all the decision-makers or input-givers are there. Then unintended consequences ensue, for example delay, confusion, frustration, or apathy.

As leaders, we need to make sure we are part of the decision-making process for strategic items, although not every single decision, which is where micromanagement lies. If we take ourselves out of the decision-making process, we don't have the right to complain about the outcome of whatever decision is made. We may say, "Oh, you can make a decision; I don't care." But after we allow someone to make the final call it is all too tempting to rush in and make changes. What we don't realize is that this undermines trust within the team we empowered to make the decision in the first place.

Try to convince others less frequently that you are right in your decision and allow them to understand and experience the consequences of their decisions for themselves. This will allow them to come to a similar conclusion but also demonstrates a level of trust. Minimize the number of times you pull the trump card on a direct report, recognizing that the more you pull that trump card, the more you undermine the trust you have with him or her.

Depending on the stakes involved in the decision, you may at times need to override their inexperienced ideas with a decision that is based on your own much deeper experience. There's certainly a time and a place to use that trump card, but only do it when it's absolutely necessary. And if you do overrule them, give a clear explanation as to why you have done so. They don't have to agree with you, but it will help if you explain your reasons. By and large, they are closer to the situation than we are, and we need to recognize and respect that. Find the tension between control and allowing somebody to succeed or fail. In doing so, you will earn their trust and they are more likely to remember the lesson in the long run.

Kicking the 'decision can' down the road isn't always a bad thing. Sometimes it is called for, and doing so actually gives you more time to think and create a better plan and strategy by delaying the decision. However, the legitimate reasons for delaying decisions only apply about ten percent of the time. Ninety percent of the time a decision needs to be made right away.

Delay is often just an excuse to avoid a decision that is the opposite of what the leader is being advised to do, and it demonstrates our inability to make decisions, even when they are vexing or complex. To avoid this delay, give others a conditional commitment rather than delaying a commitment. Break decisions apart into smaller ones to keep things moving and create a conditional decision: if *this* happens, then it is okay to do *that*.

Rather than telling them you want to wait until such-and-such happens before you make a decision, tell them that if 'X' happens rather than 'Y' they can go ahead with it.

This frees them up to move forward at a later point in time, based on that conditional decision, without asking for permission after 'X' happens, so everyone wins. The boss has peace of mind that the decision only happens if 'X' happens, and the employee doesn't have to worry about coming back to the boss for a final answer.

As a leader, this might not seem as though it will help much, but it does. The unnecessary delay of a decision often causes employees to become frustrated at best and apathetic at worst. If the latter happens, you will never know the way things need to change because people have given up trying to get your approval to change things.

If your own boss struggles with this, help him or her be less of a bottleneck causer by asking conditional, closed questions, such as: "If I get 'X' accomplished first or 'Y' person to say yes, may I pursue this change?" If you refuse to delay insignificant decisions you will end up saving time in the long run.

By all means, make decisions on less important or inconsequential issues quickly. I can't tell you how many times I have witnessed CEOs making decisions about which snacks to buy for the office. Seriously! The CEO has much more important things to decide than this.

Another one is having the senior leader decide what day the Christmas party should take place. It could just be decided that it will be the third Thursday in December each year to make it simpler. Then the leader doesn't have to bothered with the issue at all. It amazes me that some leaders want to make every decision about every little thing. I wonder why they have so many people working for them if they don't trust them to make a decision about what brand of light bulbs to purchase.

There is no substitute for a good, old-fashioned deadline that forces you to narrow your focus. Making decisions under pressure is good for leaders as it forces us to focus rather than putting things off. I do some of my best creative work when I'm under pressure from self-imposed deadlines. I find it forces me to focus and crank out work in a timely fashion. If I don't absolutely have to get something done by a certain time, an artificial, self-imposed deadline forces me to focus, and that is increasingly important when it comes to achieving productivity in our restless, technology-fueled world. We don't need the pressure of a real-life crisis to force us to make a decision. We simply need to belly up to the bar as leaders and take responsibility for providing quicker answers for our teams.

When committing to a deadline for a project that we oversee or have responsibility for, we should make sure that we set ticking time bombs. By that I mean that when we agree to do something for someone else, we should ask to commit to a timeline, either verbally or in an email, whether our bosses are imposing one or not. This opens the door for a conversation about intermediary deadlines that need to be met first in order to manage your boss' expectations by helping him or her think through a number of steps that have probably not previously been thought through.

Let's say that your deadline is sixty days from now. There are things your boss probably needs to provide before you can get started. You can explain that unless you get their commitment to receive their part (or someone else they have authority over's part) by the thirty-day mark you will be unable to complete the full project in sixty days. This really puts the ball back in their court, and if they complain that you didn't get it done in sixty days, you will be able to say that the sixty-day deadline assumed that their thirty-day deadline was met, which it wasn't. Having said that, don't wait until the sixty-day deadline is up to remind them of their thirty-day timeline.

This should not be used as an excuse to blame others when you share some of the culpability; it just means that you should be very careful in terms of how you how you structure, communicate, and follow up on these expectations. This also works in reverse. If you ask for something to be done, make sure you ask for a commitment on whatever it is they say they are going to do by a certain deadline. In doing so, you will force yourself to think things through from their perspective and appreciate the additional level of detail you probably aren't considering. Then you will have more realistic expectations of the project and a reduced chance of feeling frustrated at the end of the timeline.

Ask them what they think a reasonable timeline is without worrying about having to commit to this exactly. This shows that you respect their workload because you asked for their opinion. You can always meet in the middle if your timelines don't agree. And by all means, give your people enough time to complete their projects. Don't make every job a rush job. Some are, but they won't be overwhelmed by an infrequent rush job if it actually is infrequent.

The one downside of ticking time bomb deadlines is that people may not read the email in time, so make sure you give them enough time to read your email before you put too short a timeline on the project. Or better yet, discuss it with them in person with someone else there as a witness. At the end of the day, once they learn that you're serious about these deadlines and that you will move forward without them if you don't hear back by a certain time, they will start to pay more attention to future requests.

> "When you set yourself a goal, try to be as *specific* as possible. 'Lose five pounds' is a better goal than 'lose some weight' because it gives you a clear idea of what success looks like. Knowing exactly what you want to achieve keeps you motivated until you get there" (Heidi Grant Halvorson, taken from *Succeed: How We Can Reach Our Goals*).

When you hold brainstorming sessions, make sure they are carefully structured so you don't get lost in a quagmire, debating too many different ideas and solutions or following rabbit trails. (I like to call these 'rabid trails' because they tend to make people rabid with frustration.)

Focus on ideas that will have a low cost and high impact in your team. You can assign these to project managers with realistic timelines. This will make brainstorming sessions more productive and keep the subject matter from wandering too far off the beaten path. Part of the responsibility of a leader in calling a meeting is to ensure that the scope stays within certain constraints so that the meeting accomplishes its goal. Create an agenda for each meeting, or at least have rough boundaries in mind so that everyone is as focused, efficient, and effective as possible.

Many of us, myself included, have a tendency to wait until the last minute to decide specifically what will be on the agenda. This type of meeting is never as productive as it should be and can even be a waste of employees' precious time. So if you call a meeting, prepare, prepare, prepare, and take charge of the conversation if it veers off track.

Take notes when inspiration strikes, even if it happens in a meeting. Stop what you're doing and record it somehow. Write it down, whiteboard it (and take a picture) or dictate it into a smartphone app for transcription. I use ListNote, a free Android app, for this. Don't violate respect and etiquette for the person speaking in the meeting or your team, but find a way to jot down a brief note.

Trust me, it is worth taking the time to do this. The times that I don't, I almost always forget the creative inspiration, and then it is gone forever. I find I am most filled with creative thought during my drive to work and during meetings in which all participants are actively engaged in conversation.

11

Failure Preferred: That's What Feedback Is For

"It's not what you achieve; it's what you overcome. That's what defines your career" (former MLB catcher Carlton Fisk).

The midway point between learning from our past failures and being hopeful about the future is living in the present. I have learned way more by trying and failing than I ever have by succeeding. It seems that for most of my career I have experienced challenging work environment after challenging work environment. And while this is frustrating most of the time, I can clearly see the challenges that have prepared my path for the successes of today as I look in the rear-view mirror.

We are all bound to make mistakes. Don't fall for the lie, myth, or fallacy that you can learn enough to avoid mistakes by reading books or talking to other people or having mentors, although I do appreciate you purchasing this book! Books can have a positive benefit as they stimulate our minds to find different ways of thinking and acting, and I believe in them. They will certainly help you reduce the number of mistakes you make, but you will certainly make some mistakes.

Hopefully, you will learn from them and not make the same ones again. Part of the beauty of life and work is that even as we make mistakes (hopefully minimizing the impact of them), we learn, mature, and make better decisions in the future. Celebrities and highly respected business leaders or speakers aren't any more important or special than you and I. They also make mistakes. They may have more knowledge or wisdom based on their life experiences, but we need to be careful not to put them on a pedestal. There is no such thing as arriving at the pinnacle of success, never again a mistake to make.

The pain of your failure will be someone else's gain. In order for us to become who we want to be, we must go through peaks and valleys, and it is only through this process that we will be prepared for the journey ahead, as well as lighting the path for others, to help them avoid making the mistakes we made. Without those peaks and valleys, we would not be as useful to the people who cross our paths. Be for someone else what you wish you had in your own life. Our pain is an opportunity to help impact other people's lives for the better; they can be comforted as a result of our past pain.

> "There is only one way under high heaven to get anybody to do anything. Did you ever stop to think of that? Yes, just one way. And that is by making the other person want to do it" (Dale Carnegie, taken from *How to Enjoy Your Life and Your Job*).

If you have time to micromanage people, you won't have enough to work on your own projects, or you will become horribly out of touch with the work your team does. As a leader you can have too much time on your hands. Make sure that you have enough work to do yourself rather than just delegating everything.

The tasks you choose to involve yourself in clearly communicate what you do and don't care about. This will also communicate who you do or don't trust. It is unwise to ignore the negative effects of micromanaging. I knew of a manager in a previous company I worked for, let's call him Bob. Bob chose to focus some of his time every day on monitoring the people that indirectly reported to the manager that reported to him as they walked past his window to get coffee. This was such a waste of time, as Bob should have allowed his manager to manage his direct reports. Otherwise, why did he employ this manager?

When Bob talked to the employees' manager about his staff wasting time getting coffee every day, the staff ended up walking over to the other side of the building to get coffee so Bob couldn't see them any more. Bob thought he had fixed the problem, but his microman-agement had caused others to work around him rather than respecting him, and he wasn't self-aware enough to notice his own flaw.

Do you want people to paper over your company's problems or to let you know what they are without fear of reprisal? The extent to which you choose to micro-manage them will determine whether they obfuscate or clearly communicate the realities of your organization.

Judge performance over political clout and behavior over motives. Ensure that you are giving continuous feedback to your team based on their actual behavior and quantifiable performance, so that when they attend their formal performance reviews there are no surprises. And when you deliver that feedback, lighten up the mood with laughter where appropriate. If it is a serious matter, laughter might not be the best. Just make sure that you aren't afraid when you are delivering some 'medicine' to crack an appropriate joke. Sometimes it makes the medicine go down more easily, especially if you are dealing with tough employees. Judge your employees on both the 'means' and 'ends'. 'Means' relates to the way in which people do or accomplish something, and 'ends' relates to the actual achievement of a specific task or goal.

The tendency is to manage people based on how they carry out a task we have assigned them and whether or not they accomplished it. There are certain standards of means that we need to measure, but we can't only manage based on the means or we may end up micromanaging.

Likewise, if we only focus on the ends we may miss some of the finer details that point to poor character or disregard for standards. If you focus solely on ends, you may find that your employee is willing to manipulate the system to achieve their performance metrics in an illegal or unethical way.

By the same token, they may have missed those metrics but have a reasonable explanation as to why. Maybe they had a bad month following a string of successes or there was a certain variable they couldn't control. For instance, if you have a particularly good salesperson, your target closure ratio for them may be seventy-five percent when normally it is fifty percent.

Some people will cheat to meet the unrealistic goal by manipulating the numbers to their advantage, which meets the letter of the law but violates its spirit. On the flip side, perhaps they are not meeting their goals but, when you take the time to understand what's going on, you recognize that you have put too much on their plate. They don't have time to achieve the goal, which is to close more deals. The key factor to discern is whether the person is giving an illogical justification or a logical and reasonable explanation. The line between the two can be quite hard to see.

Avoid collective constructive correction. Never correct or rebuke an entire team of people when only one or two people need to change their behavior. Sit down privately with the one or two and have the challenging but necessary conversation. Sadly, I've seen too many managers follow the former course of action.

Ninety percent of the time you should be direct and straightforward in giving feedback to those who directly report to you as close to the event as possible, but ten percent of the time you won't want to do so because it will make the situation worse.

I once had an employee who was manipulative and passive-aggressive. Let's call her Joan. If I talked to Joan about any of her problem areas, it exacerbated the situation because she wasn't even aware of her shortcomings. She tried to manipulate me and say bad things about me to others, including human resources, in a company culture that chose to listen more to the employee than trusted managers.

Fortunately, her passive-aggressive nature was well known to my boss and to HR, so her accusations about me didn't stick. Plus, my integrity was established among leaders within the organization. But if her manipulative character hadn't been known, and I had been a newbie, I would have had a tiger by the tail, and it would have been her word against mine.

When someone owns up to their mistakes, be gracious and accept their apologies. I admit that I struggle with how to respond to an apology or an admission of guilt or forgetfulness. I usually say, "That's okay" or "I understand". What do you say as a leader? "I forgive you" sounds too formal and "I understand" might give the impression that the mistake is no big deal. You certainly don't want to say, "Thanks a lot!" or "Jerk!" or leave an awkward silence. Perhaps the best thing to say is: "I appreciate your apology. Please remember this situation so that you don't make the same mistake in the future."

Never ask an employee's peer or subordinate to monitor or assess that employee's performance. I have witnessed this, believe it or not. This is highly inappropriate, demonstrates a lack of spine, sends mixed messages, causes confusion, betrays the inherent trust in the chain of command, and ultimately undermines employee relationships. This may sound like common sense, but you would be surprised at how often I come across this egregious act.

When giving formal performance reviews, make sure that you look at those who indirectly report to you, since you can may be able to give different or affirming input. It is always good to have another perspective. This gives you, as the indirect supervisor, the opportunity to let the direct supervisor know things they might be unaware of relating to their direct report, allowing them to include this information during the review.

12

Delegation Disorder
and Title Envy

Define your authority over your direct reports or they will define it themselves. You will have no one to blame but yourself if you don't. Early in my career I was general manager of a company called Loma Lux, which sold its skincare products nationwide through Walgreens, Rite Aid, and Target. It no longer sells these products through retailers, but the company still exists online.

We had a situation with one of those retailers that caused us to seriously consider bringing a lawsuit against them. Months later, we filed a suit after we had given the decision much thought and discussion. We were a micro company compared with this retailer and the litigation dragged on for more than a year.

Then, a few weeks before it went to trial, both parties agreed to meet for a settlement conference to see whether a retired judge could help negotiate the impasse. I flew to Chicago with our company attorney and rode the elevator to a whole floor that was occupied by this company. I will admit that it was somewhat intimidating, but I was determined not to let that show.

Fortunately, we settled for an undisclosed sum of money, and I called the owner of my company to let him know. He was upset that I hadn't called him to get his permission on the amount we had settled for. I was taken aback. He had known I was taking this trip for the purpose of settling it. Yet he never asked me to call him before we made a commitment. Now, in retrospect, I probably should have given him the courtesy of a call, but I genuinely didn't think I needed to. I was the general manager and the owner hadn't personally managed the company for seven or more years.

So we need to be explicit, even when we don't think we need to be, and especially in relation to things that are of significant importance. While this whole situation was costly and stressful, none of my peers got to have this firsthand experience. It was invaluable to me and led to a growth in confidence that I could go up against a large Fortune 50 company and not die!

If we cannot leave the office and our team behind for at least a week, it should be obvious that we are not delegating tasks and empowering our teams properly. It's crucial that we do this well so that our teams can function without us. This doesn't mean they don't need us or that we don't add value to the team, but if we are doing our jobs properly as leaders we should always be replaceable. We should be training up other people who can manage the team appropriately rather than leaving them completely dependent on one leader.

Failure to do this is not true leadership; it is a fear-based excuse for leadership. Managing and leading in that way is focused on the individual rather than on what's best for the team. People who lead that way don't get the best out of their teams, and, as a result, their teams do not live up to their potential because they aren't empowered to. Leaders like this want to hoard power and knowledge so that the organization would have a hard time replacing them. Their time and energy would be better spent in sharing their wealth of knowledge with others, so much so that the organization doesn't want them to go elsewhere and share that insight with someone else's staff.

An easily glossed-over part of proper delegation is employee titles. Give employees titles that are appropriate for their positions and the size of the organization. If you're a small company, you don't necessarily want to give your accountant and your top financial person a CFO title, as this will give them a big head and make them think they should be paid more according to the average salary for that title in the job market. Perhaps a better position or title would be controller or accounting manager.

Avoid giving every Tom, Dick, and Harry a managerial title, especially if they manage no one but themselves. Use 'XYZ specialist' or 'XYZ assistant' instead. You might be thinking, "Miles, you're making a mountain out of a molehill here!" But I can tell you, from my experience, that I have seen this trip up employees and companies on many occasions. Appropriate titles, just like pay ranges, are super important in setting employee's expectations.

13

Wrap-up: Feeling Uncomfortable Yet?

"Our finest moments are most likely to occur when we are feeling deeply uncomfortable, unhappy, or unfulfilled. For it is only in such moments, propelled by our discomfort, that we are likely to step out of our ruts and start searching for different ways or truer answers" (M. Scott Peck, taken from *The Road Less Traveled*)

There are many parallels between driving and business. Many people will resent you passing them. They will temporarily speed up behind you to show you they can keep up and flip you the bird because it reminds them they aren't pressing forward towards their goals. Ignore the haters and detractors. They will give up after a short while. Keep your focus on your goals and don't let them force you off track.

Most of the frustration we have with the people that report to us stems from the myth that we believe, not explicitly but definitely implicitly, that others should act exactly like us. We all have different personalities, motivations, and life experiences; different identities. The more we try to force them to conform to our own identity, the more we hinder the productivity of the team and the growth of the organization.

We need to recognize that each person is wired differently and allow them to operate within the boundaries or parameters that we set. This gives them the freedom to pursue some of those tasks using a slightly different manner or method than you might have. If we don't, we will train them to believe that everything has to be run through the boss because he or she is the only one who can do it correctly, which results in a bottleneck and a proven lack of trust. If we continually correct their work at a gnat-sifting level, we train them to run every tiny decision through our explicit approval process. I'm not saying that we can't make changes to or have input into their work, but we have to be careful not to give too much direction, implying that they are incapable of doing the job without our overbearing hand-holding. This is a very fine line to walk.

Part 3: The Danger of 'Persona Non Grata'

Persona non grata: an unwelcome person.

Your organization's public and private persona should be the same. I once worked for an organization where the senior leader wanted any public-facing facilities to be kept up more impressively than the private ones. Believe you me, the employees that used the facilities noticed the difference in the way they were being treated.

The private facilities had well-worn carpets, dingy bathrooms, and twenty-year-old paint. I can certainly understand not wanting to spend money going overboard for our digs, but new paint, carpet, and pictures every twenty years isn't unreasonable. This cost-saving endeavor speaks volumes to the internal staff that they don't matter as much as the general public. The employees nearly lived in the facilities and some even slept there as they worked around the clock.

So consider this when you're looking to rent or lease a business premises. Consider whether the place has recently been vacant or occupied. Oftentimes, if the place has been vacant for a while it might not be the best place to rent. It may be run down or there might be other negative factors that plagued the last tenants, such as bankruptcy. Don't disregard some of the intangibles of the office environment in addition to how things physically look. Whether it was recently vacated or not, it will have implications for your organization moving forward.

Office ambiance matters as much to employees as it does to customers and donors. The building in which we work matters to our teams. Typically, we spend more time at work than we do at home, although remote working has gained ground in recent years.

It says a lot about a company if it is unwilling to invest a little bit to upgrade the inside of a building. Your buildings, wall hangings, paint, carpet, and furniture all matter. It is amazing what a new coat of paint or flooring can do for sagging morale. One of the dangers of allowing things to stay the same for twenty years is that there may still be visual reminders of better or bad times. Things have changed, and the work environment should follow suit. Some of these changes are less expensive than others, so budget can't be ignored, but don't use this as an excuse.

Be careful about trying to maintain an organization-wide public persona if it doesn't match up with the private persona. It will catch up to you eventually. This applies not just to buildings but also to our lives. We should be authentic in public about who we really are in private. If not, you or your organization will eventually be unmasked and you may find yourself labeled with the title of 'persona non grata'.

14

Courteous Communication

When people complain about a leader's lack of communication, it is less about the lack of communication and more about the offense taken and our unwillingness to admit our communication mistakes by following through on a commitment to change and improve in the future. Be concise with your words via email, text, and in person, just as people should be behind a microphone or in front of a camera.

Choose to speak with fewer, but more descriptive words so that you are as succinct and clear as possible. Loop people in on progress that affects them. It is thoughtful and will build trust if you show that you cared enough to bring them up to speed. Don't leave people wondering. Explain why you do things. This doesn't mean we have to tell them *everything*, but sometimes an extra dose of communication helps to remove doubt or suspicion.

I work from home several times a month and could easily just state that I am working from home and leave it at that, but I email my team to explain that I'm working from home because of a doctor's appointment or to visit a customer or vendor, or simply to get some work done without interruption. The point is that, in the vacuum of a lack of information, people draw the wildest of conclusions.

Some leaders hold their cards very close to their chests and choose not to communicate anything that's going on in their personal lives. Some things should be kept private, so we shouldn't tell them about too much of our leadership minutiae. But avoid the conscious or unconscious thought that we don't owe our teams anything, and before you say, "Miles, that isn't me", just take a minute to reflect on that.

Other times, common courtesy would be to ask someone, when calling them on the phone, "Hey Steve, do you have a few minutes, or are you busy?" That seems simple, right? The reality is that most people just don't do it. Take the time, be polite, and the person you are calling will most likely consider you a thoughtful person for asking. And if they are too busy, you have given them a way to politely say that they need to call you back later.

Or when you walk out of someone's office, ask them if they want their door open or shut, no matter how it was when you walked in. This shows that you are thoughtful and courteous of their preferences, especially if you opened their door in the first place. These might seem like small things, but they communicate that we are looking out for others' interests, not just our own, and have thoughtfully demonstrated that their time and space is just as valuable as your own.

Managers should measure their thoughts and actions rather than doing or saying whatever pops into their minds. We don't have the luxury of doing anything other than that because people hang on to our every word.

Make sure you are clear as to whether you are giving a suggestion or direct order when talking to subordinates. This often isn't clear to the person on the receiving end. Sometimes a leader's team discussion is simply 'spaghetti talk', where we just throw out random ideas without the intention of anyone taking action on them.

This seems simple, but I have routinely watched leaders become puzzled later in the process over why someone is working on an idea that was only casually mentioned during a team meeting. The reason is that, in the leader's head, he or she was just brainstorming, but leaders' words may have more power than they realize. If we aren't aware of this and don't become more explicit with our teams, our staff will take ideas and run with them, even if they aren't important or high priority.

One of the reasons to say no to ideas is that, if you say maybe and leave the door open for that particular idea or project, people will often run off and do it anyway. There is a lot more power in what we say than we think. People tend to react to our implications or body language even if we don't explicitly tell them to do something. One time I had a boss who said, as a side comment, that it would be nice to have some T-shirts printed for an upcoming event. So the person responsible for that kind of thing went off and did a fair amount of research on T-shirt options.

What the boss never said, and we only found out later, was that it was a really low priority. This all could have been avoided if the leader had been more cautious about his off-the-cuff comment. Sadly, we ended up spending extra time on a project that wasn't important when those resources could have been directed into more urgent projects. Eventually, people will get tired of and start trying to avoid this kind of situation if it happens repeatedly.

Don't leave your spouse in the dark about work. Some people tell their spouse or partner nothing about the challenges they're facing in their daily work lives, while others divulge everything. My advice is to find a happy medium. If you tell them nothing, they will have no idea what's going on or why you're stressed, and will be blindsided if you lose your job. At the other end of the spectrum, if you tell them everything this will overload them and then it becomes more of a challenge in your relationship because you're always complaining. Try to find a balance, demonstrating that you understand they also have frustrations in their work and personal lives. Listen to their problems; don't just tell them yours.

Neither care too much nor too little about feedback. Offer people a simple but not simplistic explanation as to why decisions are made. Don't insult people's intelligence by giving them a 'BS' answer. People aren't stupid; just explain your rationale in a way that is believable. They don't have to agree with your rationale, they just need to understand it and see it as credible.

Don't assume people will object to change by starting with an apology. Sometimes we create objections in our minds that we think other people will have. Assume that the change won't be a problem, but be ready to explain why you want to make it if the team objects.

My wife is the music and drama director at a K-12 school, and she was afraid of the students' reaction to a necessary change to rehearsal time. When she told them the basic reason they were cool with it. She had anticipated much more objection from them in her mind and realized she needn't do that in the future.

The same should apply when assuming that a vendor is out to overcharge you or that an employee will spend too much. If you won't tell somebody upfront what the budget for a particular project you're asking them to complete is, you have no business asking them what their product or service or project is going to cost. You owe it to them to tell them upfront what you think you can afford, and then they will find a way to work within that amount.

Our fear as leaders is that if we divulge our budgets the employee will overspend or the vendor will over-charge the organization. But this demonstrates a lack of trust in people. I think it is a much better solution to tell the employee or vendor what you think you can afford and start the conversation on a good note based on trust. Maybe the number you give is too high or too low, but it begins a better conversation at the beginning of the project rather than at the end, when all the research has been done and the leader who was asking for this research is frustrated with the available options and says he or she simply can't afford to follow through on it. You've just wasted a ton of this vendor or employee's time and demonstrated that you are an untrustworthy leader.

15

Pragmatic and Vulnerable, Not Idealistic and Guarded Negotiation

Vulnerability can be used as a negotiation tactic. It can disarm the other party and help you get to the heart of the matter rather than tiptoeing around things. As crazy as it might sound, try communicating to the other party that: "My biggest fear in this negotiation is _____."

You might be thinking that I have lost my mind. Yet this tactic will work if you intend to develop a long-term business relationship with another company. It acknowledges your greatest fear and frames things towards the future. Sure, they might try to take advantage of you, but that will only happen once, and I submit that to be successful in the long run you need to find solid, trusted partners to work with.

If we're always looking to get the best deal and beat the other side every single time, this will result in short-sighted wins that become fewer and farther between, since our reputation as bone-cutting negotiators will eventually proceed us. The profitable deals are nearly always come in a long-term business relationship, where our reputation for shrewd but fair negotiation rules the day.

So don't swing for the fences with every negotiation; we need to go for singles and doubles and maybe even a triple every now and again. Instead, if we always aim for the home run, we will miss many base hits that will make us successful in the long run. The dirty little secret about always going for the long ball is that it rarely happens. Sadly, this remains a fallacy in many people's minds. It's not as glamourous to focus on the fundamentals of business and getting base hits one at a time, which will gradually add up, than it is to aim for the one big thing that will take us to the top.

And don't be afraid to use the 'good cop, bad cop' routine when negotiating with customers, donors, or vendors. Now, I'm not suggesting that we try to manipulate people, but when a person calls an organization with a frustration, they will perceive that their interaction is taking place with a bad cop. This happens naturally, and the receiving customer service person won't have to try to be the bad cop. The customer or donor just focuses their frustration on the receiving front line team member. As that front line person's manager, you can usually call and resolve the issue more easily. The customer or donor sees you as the decision-maker. They have had time to cool off and rethink things, and they naturally want to see you as the good cop who can solve their problem. So run with it.

Unless you're violating your moral or ethical code, or you just want to be frustrated throughout your career, choose the pragmatic option and don't fall prey to the idealistic or supposedly principled option. While idealism has its place, it's very tricky, and our supposed principles (excluding morals and ethics) will often betray and mislead us.

There is a big difference between idealism and optimism, and some people confuse the two. You can be an optimistic and realistic person without being idealistic. We must be careful to follow a more pragmatic, practical approach. For example, I may not like the idea that I have to pay someone to do a job in a non-profit world, thinking that I should have an all-volunteer staff since it's charitable work. But pragmatically, you may have to pay some staff members in order to offer the high quality of service you need for your non-profit.

Be cautious whenever you think of an ideal situation or find yourself saying, "Oh, how I wish it were this or that way", when it clearly isn't. If you become frustrated with certain things, stop and ask yourself, "Am I thinking idealistically or pragmatically?" More often than not we will find that we are thinking idealistically. As much as we would like things to be ideal, they rarely are.

Generally speaking, thinking more pragmatically translates into generosity. One of the benefits of thinking pragmatically is that you offer the other party you are negotiating with an equal seat at the table. So, in the aforementioned scenario, most of us would like to have volunteers do the task, but the truth is that a bit of greed is revealed in that thought. So in opting to pay the person rather than relying solely on volunteers, we communicate that we value them enough to pay them. This is actually more generous than thinking that we're saving money for the non-profit by using volunteers, since we need the money to go to programs that directly help those our mission supports instead of hiring top-shelf staff who will allow us to more effectively reach our mission both in programming content and growing donations. I know it sounds counterintuitive, but we can always raise more money. Finding and retaining a committed team is much more difficult.

One time I had a volunteer build something for an event (let's call him Bill), and then he came back and wanted to be paid for it. This was after Bill had told me upfront that he wanted to donate his time and materials. Bill was adamant that he wanted to be paid for the materials, at least. The bottom line is that I would have been justified in saying, "Too bad. You said that your time and materials were donated."

Pragmatically, I sought to find a middle ground. I ended up paying him a sum of money that we could both agree on. It wasn't as much as Bill wanted, but it was somewhere in the middle. Did I have to do that? No. Idealistically, he had told me that he was giving it to us for free. Pragmatically, I chose to make the situation easier on both of us. The organization saved face publicly and Bill was able to recoup some of his costs. He had probably committed to something without fully counting the out-of-pocket costs in addition to his time.

For customer service issues, first give the customer service department the opportunity to put the problem right. If this doesn't produce the desired effect, go straight to the top. This usually results in a swift and favorable response.

Perhaps you have an issue with a business that is not giving you the satisfaction you are looking for. You may want them to reduce your bill or give you some sort of concession. The best thing to do is go to their website, especially with a large company, and look for their head marketing person (chief marketing officer or director of marketing communications). These people don't want bad press from a disgruntled customer. You could even go to the investor relations page and find an email address on a press release.

Nine times out of ten, I have gotten exactly what I've asked for, or pretty close to it, when I've done this. I've never been completely ignored or told I can't get a resolution for my issue, as often happens with a regular customer service representative. Appeal to Caesar (metaphorically speaking), making your case to a high-level executive, and you will almost always receive a favorable resolution.

Based on the decision I made with Bill, you might say, "Miles, you're soft; you're not a strong negotiator." I disagree. In the long run, pragmatic negotiation is far better than idealistic, greedy negotiation because of the long-term implications. If you really stop to think about it, this concept has many applications in everyday life as well as in business. If you take the approach of giving the other party a little more benefit of the doubt and more negotiating room, you will come out further ahead in the long run because of those trusted relationships and the fact that some people will end up doing more for you than they would ever otherwise do.

In the short run, sure, you won't be as far ahead, but that's okay because you now know the true character of those companies and can avoid them. I usually think about the long run, not about tomorrow or this year, but about ten, twenty, thirty, or even fifty years into my career and life. My aim is to be actively engaged, giving more than I receive, and allowing others to have more of a say in the negotiating process, especially if I am in a position of negotiating strength.

16

Asynchronous Communication in the Digital Age

While the trajectory of technological advancement has made workers generally more efficient, it has created an asynchronous information problem. In our increasingly digital age, it becomes harder and harder to have synchronous communication, which for centuries was mostly face-to-face or more recently by telephone. Asynchronous communication, such as text, email, social media, and voicemail, has allowed us to leave digital messages for someone to read or listen to later.

This presents challenges in ensuring that the information is acted upon by the receiver, as they can always choose to ignore the message. The same has always been true with face-to-face or phone communication, although those people had to lie to us first. Asynchronous communication presents both a challenge and an opportunity. The opportunity is that it requires the sender of that information to stay on top of, and to be more vigilant and intentional about, following up and making sure that the necessary action is taken.

Be careful how you use the internet at work and how you use social media wherever you are. You never know what your employers or potential employers are able to see, and they have every right to keep tabs on you. They want to make sure that trade secrets, intellectual property and the like are not being disseminated electronically. I know many of us use social media for everything in our lives, but we should be cautious about what we post.

As far as personal use of the company internet is concerned, many of us are unaware that our employers can and do track that usage. Watch what emails you have coming to your work address. Many people have personal messages coming in to their work email, even messages related to secret job searches. Or they have other types of personal email arriving in their business email inboxes (ones they wouldn't want their employers reading), mistakenly assuming that their employers have no access to their emails.

Most of the time, your employers will not be actively reading your emails, but they certainly have access and a right to read any or all of those emails any time they want, since it is their property. Just don't make any assumptions in this area. Imagine that everything you get through your work email is being read by your boss (even though it isn't), and that should help you identify what should and should not be arriving in your inbox.

I once had an indirect report who accidentally sent me a personal email intended for a friend of hers. She proceeded to tell me how she had consumed quite a bit of alcohol, got drunk, and had an 'awesome make-out' session with her boyfriend. "Oops" is right. We should keep our work email accounts for work only, since our employers own our business email, web searches, and any other activity completed on their network, including personal stuff we access on our mobile phones if they are connected to the company's internet.

While we're on the subject of email, let's discuss email etiquette. Refrain from using too many smiley faces or unreadable backgrounds in your business emails. Use the CC function to ensure that there is good communication among many relevant people but never as a tool to bust or rat on someone. Rarely, if ever, BCC someone; that's just covering your own butt or trying to rat someone out without being a grown up about it. Personally, I think we should ban BCC, since we shouldn't use it unless we are willing to use CC. The only exception is if there was a serious legal or ethical issue; then BCC might be okay. Be careful with CC and more so with BCC as it may appear that you are trying to get someone into trouble. Instead, go talk to the person. If it happens repeatedly and they won't stop, talk to your boss verbally, not via BCC.

17

Anything You Can Do, I Can Do Better?

In order to be effective in leadership, we absolutely have to have a certain level of ego. We can't expect people to follow someone who doesn't, at some level, believe they are smarter or more talented than others. The real challenge and the key to being truly successful in life and leadership is to keep enough of that ego in check, so that it doesn't turn us into unreasonable, dictatorial tyrants. We need to use ego when it is needed, without allowing it to control us or dominate the people we lead. Our posture and approach should always be one of giving others what they need, not necessarily what they want, and doing what is best for the organization.

Leaders bring things to a conclusion, but not necessarily to a consensus. If consensus can be obtained relatively quickly in tandem with conclusion, all the better. Waiting to find consensus on every issue usually takes much longer when swift decisions need to be made that not everyone is going to agree with. It is a double-edged sword. Swift decisions that aren't popular with everyone are decisive and clear but can lead to bad consequences, while delayed decisions, used to gain one hundred percent support, might eventually lead to positive outcomes but at the time may be perceived as an inability to make a decision when all the chips are on the table.

Following a populist approach by gaining unanimous consensus can also be dangerous in the sense that the entire team may strongly believe a particular action is required when you can see that they are falling prey to groupthink. Alternatively, the majority of people may believe that something needs to be changed or fixed, while one or two key people have detailed, intimate, strategic knowledge on the topic and do not see things the same way as everyone else. So be careful if you're primarily using consensus to identify problems or challenges within the organization.

"We can't lead others where we haven't been."

Ken Jennings, CEO of US locksmith company Mr. Rekey, rates leaders on a scale of one to ten, with ten being the most skilled, wise, and adept leader. Most people will only hire leaders that are at their level, or one or more levels below them. If you are a level three leader you tend to hire ones, twos, or threes. Then you mature into a five and you are able to recognize and hire level three and four leaders.

The downside is that you then have level one, two, or three leaders on your team, and if they don't mature at the same pace as you, you will have to make changes. However, many leaders stick with team members who refuse to grow, believing that they are remaining loyal to those who have been with them through thick and thin. We certainly want loyalty in our teams, especially if they have proved their mettle in the past, but if they get stuck at a plateau and won't budge, even with our encouragement, we need to help them move on.

Likewise, if we are frustrated with our team of levels one to three, and are now a level five ourselves, that is on us as leaders. Solid leaders will outgrow their people, but we must help and encourage others to grow as we do. Some employees will choose to stay at the same level, so hire and retain people who will grow and adapt alongside you.

> "'Welcome, Prince,' said Aslan. 'Do you feel yourself sufficient to take up the Kingship of Narnia?'
>
> 'I - I don't think I do, Sir,' said Caspian. 'I am only a kid.'
>
> 'Good,' said Aslan. 'If you had felt yourself sufficient, it would have been proof that you were not.'"
>
> (C.S. Lewis, taken from *Prince Caspian*.)

Don't fall for the lie that you did the best you could in any particular situation. It is an insidious lie, and one that we could tell ourselves every day if we're not careful. The truth is that I often could have done better as a leader and, in hindsight, I owe it to my team to learn, grow, and be better the next time.

We even make this excuse for others, saying: "Sally did the best she could." I don't even want other people to say that I did the best I could, because I know that's not true. I could have done better. I could have worked harder. I could have been smarter. I could have done things differently. Keep this in mind and you will naturally stretch yourself and grow continuously.

> "Aslan: 'Rise, Kings and Queens of Narnia.'
>
> [Peter, Edmund, and Susan stand up, but Caspian stays, head bowed, on one knee.]
>
> Aslan: 'All of you.'
>
> Prince Caspian: 'I do not think I am ready.'
>
> Aslan: 'It's for that very reason, I know you are.'"
>
> (C.S. Lewis, taken from *Prince Caspian*.)

Being in charge or in leadership comes with a certain level of authority. So, naturally, we tend to give more credence to our own ideas and more skepticism to others' ideas. We need to be very careful about recognizing our own bias towards our ideas and intentionally giving the opposite view its due.

Try to talk others out of your ideas, since they will often want to follow whatever you say because you are the boss. We have to guard against this natural bias of desiring others to validate rather than challenge our ideas. Often they could talk us out of a bad idea for reasons we hadn't considered, while at others times we need to charge ahead even though others say we shouldn't. Just make sure you slow down long enough to ask others to take the opposing view and help you see the other side of the coin first. You will be glad you did.

Give your team space to express their negative emotions about frustrations they have at work. Make your time with them a safe place. Don't chastise them or avoid topics that are uncomfortable, particularly if you are the source of their pain. As leaders and managers, we should almost never make somebody feel fearful of losing their job. Fear is a powerful demotivator, so be careful if you are trying to use it to motivate someone as it usually does the opposite. It will also make them second guess themselves on every future decision, and not in a positive way. You are likely unaware of the unintended consequences: that your actions are causing others to hide things and lie to you. If you threaten people's jobs over a performance issue, they can go into a shell-shocked state that is counterproductive and is likely to become a self-fulfilling prophecy.

If you think you know how to do someone else's job better than they do, you probably don't. You don't know what you don't know. If we have never done a particular job or a particular task and are asking someone else to do it, we have to be very careful not to set our expectations too high. This even applies if we have done the job or task ourselves in the past.

That's not to say that we can't have high standards that we expect others to stick to, but I have found in my own life that I tend to have expectations that are too high, and I either have to choose to lower those expectations or be continually disappointed. We do need to challenge the team or individual with the project or task we are asking them to do, but be reasonable and understand that our natural inclination as leaders is to have overly high expectations. I cannot overstate the fact that there is a very fine line between expectations that are too high and too low.

The most dangerous leaders are the ones who used to have knowledge and understanding of a particular position, department, or industry, but have been elevated to a higher role in the organization with direct oversight over the position, department, or industry in which they used to have expertise. The longer the time and further away a person gets from that first-hand knowledge, the greater the chance that they won't realize how much things have changed. These days things are changing even more rapidly, which is making the situation worse.

Often decisions are made based on months-old or sometimes even years-old information, which may result in dangerous or even disastrous consequences. We may think we know what's going on and as a result want to have more input, but we must realize that this is a dangerous path because it relies on old data and information.

Nowhere is this more critical than in the area of business consultant overreach. Keep external consultants on a very short leash and timeline, since they may have a limited understanding of your specific situation. They aren't working in the day-to-day operations and are likely to gloss over certain important considerations.

The challenge is that, if you keep them on longer term, this has a tendency to cause confusion among your staff because they don't know whether the owner, direct supervisor, or consultant is directing their daily actions. It becomes problematic as it sends mixed messages, not to mention the fact that consultants are brought in to give us new ideas and plans but are rarely the implementers of the plan. So the longer they are there, the more likely they are to charge you fees for things you either don't need or haven't asked for.

Keep the scope of what you're asking them to do limited, guard against scope creep, and let them know you want to hear their plans, which you will take responsibility for executing. If you want to hire them to implement the actions, bring them on board as employees with specific, limited authority and a definite end date so that everybody knows where they stand. But don't confuse the issue, especially by allowing consultants to stay on too long or by having multiple consultants at the same time. This will cause all kinds of problems and misunderstandings about who is really in charge.

18

Avoid an Assumption-Fueled, Bigger Mess of a Mistake

There is a fine line when it comes to maintaining a healthy level of respect between leader and team member. And, as leaders, we cannot manage our teams' reactions to our actions completely. But if there was no need to do a good job in order to get good performance reviews and requisite pay increases, we wouldn't be motivated to work efficiently and effectively.

Not wanting to lose faith and trust with your boss is a far cry from how some organizations work. In some workplaces there is a high level of fear on a daily basis as people are genuinely worried that they might lose their job that day if they inadvertently say the wrong thing to the boss. Or maybe they may not necessarily lose their job, but they are uncertain of their boss' mood from day to day, since he or she is so emotionally unpredictable. This is the worst characteristic of a boss, since you never know whether you are going to get Dr. Jekyll or Mr. Hyde on any given day. It is sad that so many leaders manage in this way.

I have known a couple of managers like this. They do well emotionally for a while, but then they get upset, overreact, and blow up, leaving all kinds of chaos in their wake, all because they don't know how to handle challenging times or frustrating emotions. Then they go back to acting like everything is great. Employees tire quickly of an unpredictable boss. They don't know if today is *the day*. If we approach our employees in a way that causes them to be fearful of losing their jobs, we are not exhibiting servant leadership.

If we hold people accountable in an appropriate way and they have a healthy level of respect for us and for the job they do, knowing that they need to do a good job, that's okay. Just don't use your authority as an excuse to hold people to an unattainable level of accountability, even by your own personal standards, as they may not be as efficient as you are. Added to this, you might only be able to afford a certain level of productivity, so consider whether your pay range fits your expectations.

I have often heard overbearing managers say, "Well I'm just holding people accountable" when they're clearly asking for perfection. This is taking things to an extreme that the manager himself or herself cannot achieve, even though he or she really thinks it's attainable. Some of this has to do with being many years removed from doing the front-line work that someone else is now doing. Maybe you've lost sight of the increasingly challenging nature of the work or the additional duties and responsibilities that have been added since you moved up the ladder.

I try to give employees the benefit of the doubt unless they are obviously very lazy. Usually that is not the case, and if they say they could get a task done if they weren't so overwhelmed I will take their word for it until proven otherwise. Ninety percent of the time we underestimate the amount of work it takes for our employees to complete a singular task. It just comes with the leadership territory. The further removed we are from that work, the more distant our understanding will be. So be very cautious. This is a big trap that many leaders fall into.

Are you an over-reactor or an under-reactor? In either case, you may need to temper what you say to your boss in terms of how your team is performing. I am a bit of an over-reactor, but only in my mind. To the everyday observer, I am cool, calm, and collected on the outside. My tendency is to want to say that things are a bit worse than they are because I'm a cautious optimist. But I've learned how to temper my thoughts before they come out as words. Other people may have the exact opposite issue to watch out for. Either way, if we aren't careful we can make a bigger mess of a mistake.

When I was a teenager, I wore a baseball hat to a youth symphony rehearsal and the conductor (let's call him Jimmy) embarrassed me in front of the entire orchestra by demanding that I remove it in the middle of the rehearsal. There were no rules about wearing hats, and even if there had been Jimmy could have easily pulled me aside during a break and asked me to remove it and not wear it in the future. I can only guess that Jimmy assumed that my wearing the hat was disrespectful and defiant in some way. Needless to say, I was quite hurt by the public rebuke given the fact that I did not have a rebellious bone in my body towards Jimmy.

If we are far too quick to judge a situation and therefore overreact to a mistake – even a large one that we think justifies an overreaction – when we don't have the full picture, we may want to get rid of the culprit (or whoever we perceive to be the culprit) even if they perform well otherwise. If you go ahead and fly off the handle, this will even affect staff retention among those who are not caught in the cross hairs. And God forbid that your overreaction happens online, as those outbursts never go away.

Yet mistakes should be forgotten with time as we all make mistakes, even large ones at times. Often a major mistake happens after a history of positive risks that have paid off are taken, yet this one time it didn't offer a return or it caused embarrassment for the board or organization. Or it could be a moral failing. The challenge is that when these things happen, most reject, forget, or negate all of our preceding good actions. We need to allow our leaders to fail without fearing for their jobs.

"Action followed by reaction is much better than inaction followed by reaction."

Don't assume that someone knows something. You might be saying to yourself, "Thanks, Captain Obvious. I know, I know." But people don't know what they don't know, and if we assume otherwise, my fifth-grade teacher said that we are showing ourselves to be the first three letters of the word 'assume'.

Early on in my career, in around 2004, I was new to using email and genuinely didn't know that it was best practice to put a subject line in the subject line box. After I emailed someone at work (let's call her Sue), she got very mad at me for leaving all of my previous subject lines blank. She wrote a scathing reply telling me this and, needless to say, I was taken aback.

We have all been there at some point in time when we were green and naive, so we should appreciate, not assume, that others know such and such. If Sue had taken a different approach and asked me why I had left all of my subject lines blank, I would have come to the realization myself and started adding them. I *never* forget to enter a subject line when sending an email these days.

"Don't throw the baby out with the bathwater" (taken from *Narrenbeschwörung* (*Appeal to Fools*) by Thomas Murner).

I would also caution people about making vows to themselves about what they would do differently or change if they were in charge. This can take many forms, but the most common form goes something like this: "When I'm in charge, I'm never going to do X, Y, or Z."

The danger in making a vow like this is that it triggers something inside us that is 'anti' something else, and we don't even realize the implications until months or years later when we are actually in a position of power and have the authority to *never* do that thing. Then, in our effort not to do it, we go the opposite way and often overcorrect, causing just as many problems as we perceived our boss to be making, and going in the opposite direction, which is equally bad.

For example, some people who have had bosses that would yell, scream, and throw things at them may choose to be so mealy-mouthed themselves that no one respects their leadership because they are pushovers, all in their misguided efforts not to do what they had seen in their own leaders.

19

Wrap-up: Appropriate Relationship Separation

Should I take the time to earn the trust of my boss, peers, and subordinates, or do I allow the drive for results to run over people? It's not a question of one or the other, but both. There are leaders who are good at building relationships and those that are good at getting things done, and in some cases both apply.

If you're good at one and not the other, work at the one you're not good at to become a more complete leader, since effective leadership requires building accountable, trustworthy relationships that will encourage others to follow us. Great leaders understand the tension between the two when it comes to achieving goals and objectives. What makes you good at business doesn't necessarily make you good at relationships.

I've heard some people say that they wish their spouse and children would act like employees and kowtow to their every request at home. Well, personal relationships don't work that way, and it can bruise the ego when we realize that our families aren't as enamored with us as our teams are because our families don't have the threat of a loss of paycheck (however implied this is) to keep them in line.

This can also cause us to retreat from family relationships and to run to unhealthy relationships with coworkers or subordinates. It's good to get close but not too close to your direct reports and peers. The former is perhaps more dangerous politically. This could simply be a strong friendship or, in extreme cases, a sexual affair. If you end up in a romantic relationship with a co-worker, that isn't as egregious as it would be with a direct report, unless you are married. Most companies have policies that prohibit supervisors carrying on romantic or sexual relationships with direct reports.

I am a regular churchgoer, and if I have others that work for or with me who like to attend church, I usually don't like to go to the same church because we have less separation in our personal lives, which can skew my professional, objective judgment of their work performance. You may say, "Well, Miles, I don't believe in that church stuff." If so, the same goes for other activities outside of work, like being in the same softball team, bowling league, or golf group.

We want to be careful that we don't get too close personally and cross that very fine line between personal and professional. You want to have some likability with your team but still be professional enough to hold them accountable for goals and objectives. There are those who take being friends with their employees to an extreme. This results in paternalism within an organization, where no one can get fired because they are viewed as family. I submit that 'team-ism' should be the goal instead of 'family-ism'.

Teams can encourage and hold others accountable in a healthy way (not a dictatorial way), which may on occasion lead to dismissal. Paternalistic families can't bring themselves to do that. Organizations that are paternalistic in this new economy will eventually suffocate in a sea of competition, and increased efficiency and productivity.

Part 4: Fierce Competition Steamrolls Ahead

Work smarter *and* harder, because I can assure you that the competition you need to be worried about is doing both. Following the downturn of 2008, the competitive landscape changed forever. We can no longer slowly acquire and assimilate new knowledge. If we do, we risk becoming dinosaurs. Speed to market is so crucial these days, and so is continuously making your own work and your team's work more efficient. Getting more done in less time is simply a fact that we all need to not only accept but embrace because dinosaur teams and organizations die much faster these days than they did a decade ago.

Has your boss ever asked you, "What have you done for me lately?" I don't know if you have ever had this literally or figuratively asked of you, but it can be pretty demoralizing if you have. While this can be taken to a negative extreme where people fear for their jobs on a daily basis, there should be a healthy, implied expectation (never verbalized) of improved performance in some way every day.

Frankly, organizations are more reluctant to let mediocre performers skate by these days due to more aggressive competition and narrower margins in the marketplace; one positive benefit of the current, tough, economic environment. We should have enough respect for ourselves and others to find ways to continuously improve ourselves and to expect our teams to improve.

There is always an unanticipated trade-off associated with convenience, and regularly revisiting organizational strategy is no different. It is much easier, in the short term, to work 'in' the business and not enough 'on' the business. We think it is more convenient because we don't have to do the initial hard work, but in the long run our competitors will eat us for lunch because they are working to become more efficient and effective every single day.

So, are you short or long-term minded? Do you focus on managing smaller things but miss the bigger picture? Smaller things matter, but not at the expense of strategic, tectonic shifts that are taking place in nearly every industry, even in the non-profit world. It is best to set our sights on long-term objectives such as dramatically improving customer service or growing effective digital marketing to crush the competition over micromanaging small-expense items. There are two types of manager: cost-cutters and revenue growers. Be more of the latter or both, but not only the former. Your career trajectory will thank you for this later.

20

Constant Flux Demands Pig-Pen Leadership

What is Pig-Pen leadership? Within a few weeks of starting at a new company, one of my direct reports (let's call her Mary) blurted out her realization that I was a bit like Pig-Pen of *Peanuts* fame. After I got over the initial shock of being called Pig-Pen and understood what she meant, I affirmed Mary's observation, since I recognized that I do like to stir things up. I am a change agent, not for change's sake but to kickstart momentum which can lead to growth in an organization. It's just in my blood, and while I used to be ashamed of that bent, I now embrace my uniqueness.

Now, I am not recommending that you are so dirty you have a dirt cloud following you wherever you go. I am suggesting that we all need a bit of metaphorical Pig-Pen in our leadership in order to change and adapt to the unrelenting state of flux in the world today.

The challenge with starting in a new leadership role is determining how much or little change to apply, especially in the first three, six, or even twelve months. Just like an emergency room doctor, you have to quickly assess and understand what condition the patient (organization or department) is in. If the patient is on life support and in dire need of drastic changes, you must act quickly. However, if you act too quickly you may win the battle but lose the war in terms of gaining trust with your team. They may quickly lose confidence in you if you are too hasty.

"Just because it ain't broke doesn't mean it doesn't need fixing."

I'm sure that many of you reading this have heard the opposite of this quote before: "If it ain't broke, don't fix it." That couldn't be more wronger (sic). This statement is used as an excuse to avoid painful discussions about what may need to change in order for the organization to grow. In most organizations, there are things that need to be changed, but you have to be careful about changing too much too quickly. So tread lightly and be very careful, but don't be fearful of change either. It's all about finding a balance.

Note that there is a big difference between 'can't change' and 'shouldn't change'. We shouldn't use 'can't' as an excuse not to make a change, but maybe we 'shouldn't' change certain elements for a valid reason. The latter is different from throwing up our hands with the excuse that we *can't* change.

We should feel just as uncomfortable in the good times, when our organizations are doing well financially, as we do when things are going poorly. We know we need to make changes when things are going poorly. The latter certainly makes problems easier to spot, but it is very difficult when things are going well to continually strive to do better.

It's at these times that organizations tend to get fat, dumb, and happy. They start to relax a little bit. But we need to be disciplined enough to stay appropriately dissatisfied with the status quo, even if the company is trending positively. During times of plenty, we need to be diligently staying on top what is happening in our industries as well as on the front lines of our organizations. If we don't, the waves of competition will overtake us much more quickly than before.

"There's a big difference between dissatisfaction with the status quo and discontentment."

Strategic change is still needed in organizations on an ongoing basis, but the old plan of a five or ten-year strategic plan just doesn't hold water any more. The business environment is changing so quickly that those five and ten-year plans can become shackles in a jiffy. I propose that we have strategic, adaptable action plans so that we can adapt to fast-changing environments instead of sticking to formal, long-range strategic planning. This continual process should become part of the ethos and rhythm of any organization that is looking to succeed.

Sometimes change is needed at an organizational level. A reorganization can involve dramatically re-envisioning the organizational chart, marketing strategy, or something else. But recognize that strategic reorganization shifts power from certain people and departments to others. So some will be happy while others will be angry and resistant. Don't underestimate this as most leaders do. Prepare for it by planning how you will respond. This has tremendous power to affect change and restart momentum where it has been lost. Just bear in mind that some will react to that proposed change out of fear.

"Blue ocean strategy doesn't aim to out-perform the competition. It aims to make the competition irrelevant by reconstructing industry boundaries." (taken from blueoceanstrategy.com).

Finding a niche, untapped market may sound like a pipe dream. But it is more important than ever before now that mass marketing is 'mostly dead', to use the words of Miracle Max from *The Princess Bride*. There are still hundreds, maybe even thousands of unserved and underserved markets out there, but as more people realize this, these windows will rapidly close.

Even if you are in an existing, mature market, authors W. Chan Kim and Renée Mauborgne contend in their book, *Blue Ocean Strategy*, that creating a new market where there isn't one is the path to fastest growth. Chobani, the Greek yogurt company, followed a blue ocean strategy. It created a market for Greek yogurt in America, where there previously was none.

We do have to be careful not to be too early to a market, since doing so could lead to failure, but with the right timing it can really help to get there first. Another example of blue ocean strategy is to find a new way of positioning your existing product or service in a market that has almost no competition.

21

Babies Don't Always Grow Up to Be Businessmen

"Mammas Don't Let Your Babies Grow Up to Be Cowboys." (Song title written by Ed Bruce and performed by Waylon Jennings and Willie Nelson.)

It is sad but true that many business people have no business being in business. What I mean by this is that most small business leaders really don't know how to professionally manage their organizations. Yep, I said it. They have been fortunate to have had some opportunities to get a business started, or to manage or take over one, and I don't want to discount all of their success, but it is usually through the sheer force of will of others on their team that their companies survive and grow. This often happens at the expense of other people in the leader's personal life – their friends and family – whom they ignore in order to build their businesses. Alternatively, they may mistreat the people who work for them.

These are not truly business-minded professionals. They don't know how to run their operations effectively, efficiently, or professionally. Instead, they run their businesses as a way of supporting their personal financial needs, tastes, and wants, as opposed to doing what's best for the interests of the organization. It's a sad fact that many people are focused more on personal financial gain than on what's best for the company.

Many of us assume that owners and leaders have earned their positions of power. This is not always the case. Luck or serendipity has vaulted many into their positions of authority, and they really don't know how to manage an organization well; from people to finances to revenue growth to profit margins. Their weaknesses can weigh heavily on the organization and may stunt company growth. We need to be aware of this and not get too frustrated. We have to recognize that some owners, managers, and leaders shouldn't be in charge. Focus on how you can become a better leader and lead others to become better leaders themselves.

"If you don't have paying customers, you have a hobby."

The difference between an entrepreneur and a business person is that the latter knows how and when to lose money or cut losses and move on. Many people who call themselves business owners hold on to their business for far too long, viewing it as their baby rather than rationally viewing its performance and making rational, financial business decisions. So maybe you need to kill your entrepreneurial baby.

Something that has made entrepreneurship more difficult is that, in a robust, growing economy, which we enjoyed in the 1990s and even a little in the early 2000s, a mediocre leader could get away with it, have some success and be modestly profitable. By contrast, in a very tight economy like the one we have been experiencing for the last decade, the wheat is being separated from the chaff. Many who are pretending to be leaders have done badly in this economy. It will continue to be more challenging for leaders going forward, so you will have to be sharper; more on top of your game. The days of being mediocre and lucking into success are pretty much over until we experience booming economic conditions again.

"Be a growth leader, not a cost manager."

You certainly need to keep track of costs and make sure things don't get out of line with your budget, but the majority of your time should be focused on how to grow revenues or donations, and then on minimizing costs. Too many people try to cut their way to a profit, and that works initially. But you can only cut so many expenses before you start growing revenues. It's simple math that many just don't get. Maybe it seems easier and gives the manager more of a sense of control to reduce expenses. Growing revenues is harder and less certain, but doing so through aggressive sales and marketing efforts is vital if you want to keep your business going.

"Bootstrap like crazy when building a business because it will take longer than you ever planned to achieve sustainable cash flow."

Don't underestimate the amount of capital and cash flow required not only to sustain your business but to grow it. This is often called the 'cash flow shuffle'. Part of our role as leaders is to continually be aware of cash flow, ensuring that we're not spending too much or too little to grow the business. Many entrepreneurs and small business leaders underestimate the amount of capital it takes to grow a company and either pull too much money out of the business to benefit themselves personally or don't inject enough capital into it to help it grow. That goes for inventory and marketing dollars, among many other things, where the timing of cash is affected due to a delay in collecting payments after sales occur.

Cash flow is king. Amass it like it's going out of style and guard it, but don't hoard it too much. Cash flow spent on strategic, growth-focused objectives is the lifeblood of your business. Don't be fooled; sales are not. Sales *can* turn into cash flow, but only if we collect on our accounts receivable balance. Otherwise, sales do us no good. Don't misunderstand me; we have to generate sales on a consistent basis every month to survive. But we must turn those sales into cash flow and protect that cash so that we can spend it on strategic objectives.

If you understand the ins and outs of accrual accounting versus cash accounting, you will see how you need to plan for cash needs that are higher during certain times of the year (even if sales are high during the same period) so that you don't run out of cash at a crucial time for your organization, even if your financial statements appear flush with cash. Sadly, most people don't understand this concept until it's too late, and they either go bankrupt or have to settle for unfavorable loan terms just to stay afloat.

Don't fall prey to the myth that if only you had more money in your budget you could accomplish so much more and achieve much greater profits. I have worked with many organizations, both volunteer and paid, where this often comes into play. This leads to a frustration that we are not able to achieve a certain level of sales or profit, or we feel stuck in some areas. The answer is rarely just more money, which would not necessarily solve the fundamental issues. Don't get me wrong, money can help, but it's not the complete solution we often think it is.

Another critical financial mistake leaders make is in overpricing or underpricing their products and services. There are two main ways to do this, using either market pricing or cost-plus pricing methodologies. Cost-plus pricing simply takes the entire cost of creating the product or service and adds a margin on top, say five, ten or twenty percent. The downside in that this doesn't factor in what the market wants or has the ability to pay. Market pricing focuses on achieving the biggest margin from the sale that the market will bear, which either achieves a better overall margin or indicates that this might not be a market that is profitable enough to enter.

A cost-plus pricing model is okay, since it ensures that there will be some profit, but it often leaves money on the table when the market would be willing to pay more for a superior product that has no competition. A cost-plus pricing model is prevalent in manufacturing circles, where leaders try to attain a certain margin above all fixed and variable costs. However, this can be very misleading if the market is capable of bearing higher prices.

If you are using market pricing, this will help in two areas. First, you will be able to charge more for certain products in certain industries as people will be more willing to pay for them. This is a consequence of competition and scarcity. Second, if you find out that the retail price your market is willing to pay doesn't allow you enough margin, you don't even need to spend the research and development dollars to create the product.

What the item costs you to make is almost irrelevant in terms of what the market will pay for it. Start with the market then look at costs to determine whether the margin is viable; not the other way around. Take a look at what a customer might be prepared to pay for that product. Ask yourself, "What is the true value of this product or service on the open market?" Then price your products and services accordingly.

Admittedly, pricing isn't an exact science as it involves the psychology of human behavior, which influences buying, so you may have to research your competitors and do some testing. But if we use only a cost-plus approach, we may overprice or underprice our products, which will not lead to maximized profits. If we choose to price our products competitively in line with the market, or in some cases at a premium to the market – with a clear value proposition that differentiates us from our competitors – we are likely to attain a higher profit margin than we otherwise would.

Now, I have only discussed two main pricing models, but there are many variations of the market pricing model (for example bundling, target return, value-based, demand-based, competition-based, and variable), all of which have their pros and cons. Check out Rafi Mohammed's *The 1% Windfall: How Successful Companies Use Price to Profit and Grow* in order to gain insight into how you should price your product or service. He also writes a regular column in the *Harvard Business Review*, which has always provided me with thought-provoking insight.

22

Reject the Myths of the Masses... Starting with PI

Mmm. Pie. Nope, I'm not talking about apple or cherry pie, although those are tasty! I'm referring to perfect information. We may believe the myth that we can gather enough data to establish perfect information from which to make a decision, but it just doesn't happen. Beware the allure of PI. It is elusive; a siren call. Pure objectivity doesn't exist either. It is a fallacy; a red herring. We should strive for objective rather than subjective decision-making, but there is always a human element; a subjective part of the decision that has to be made.

So should we follow our gut instincts or data? I'll let you in on a little secret. That was a trick question. It should be both. Developing your business instinct or 'gut' has more to do with reviewing data as opposed to gut feel based on what we think happened. Now, data is still imperfect and should be combined with instinct, but it should not be substituted entirely.

People who trusts their gut feel completely are less credible than those who take a deep dive into the data, analyzing and drawing conclusions based on their professional experience. We need to discern how people are making their decisions and determine whether the process is based on sound data and experience from the past or whether it's just someone thinking they have the right answer based on hubris rather than data or experience.

Multitasking is yet another seductive myth. Did you know that our brains only have the capacity to think about one thing at a time? You can single-task very quickly and jump back and forth between many different items in your mind, which is what most people call multitasking. And while, generally speaking, women are better at this than men, there are men who are better at it than women. I happen to be one of those men, while my wife openly struggles rapid single-tasking.

I like to call what I do well 'sequential single-tasking'. Sequential single-tasking is the unique ability to single-task quickly by juggling many different duties, tasks, responsibilities, or projects at a time. People who have a hard time with this can be easily overwhelmed by having too many things going on, while other people thrive on it. The fact that someone can seemingly multitask a whole range of things at precisely the same time is impossible, inaccurate, and misleading. But some can do sequentially single-tasking very quickly and effectively.

"'Someday' is a dangerous word."

I want to caution you to cut the word 'someday' from your vocabulary. We often use it as an excuse that 'someday' we will do this or that. "Someday I'll learn how to paint. Someday I'll write a blog. Someday I'll do something meaningful with my life. And while this may sound like semantics, I would encourage you to start using the words 'one day' in its place.

The only reason I suggest this is to remind ourselves that when we say, "One day I will do this or that", we are making a commitment not to let ourselves off the hook. It is a way to anchor our thinking to a new mooring. Far too often we say, "Well I'm going to do this or that", because there is an emotional pay-off to impress people. Others may think, "Wow, he's going to write a book or travel to India", but we rarely check to see whether that person follows through. If we are intellectually honest with ourselves and others, we often don't have any serious plans to do those things. I would challenge us all to be doers, not just talkers.

Using one day in place of someday will help you stay awake mentally and think differently, so that you actually do more of what you say. Stop being afraid and start 'shipping' something. For years, I struggled with entrepreneurial ideas that I just talked about. Then once I had decided to write my first book I suddenly gained momentum. I still had to work at shipping my next item, consistent blog posts, but I gathered energy from each successive step. It gets so much easier the second time you do it. It's not complicated; it just takes hard work and discipline. Push your ideas out into the real world, and sure, you will receive criticism of your work, but I would rather be that person than the one who never has the guts to risk his reputation.

I have had many people ask me, "How do you have a job, a wife and three children, and still have time to write books and speak at events?" My reply is, "With discipline and endless iteration, sprinkled with regular breaks and vacations." I would much rather live an ordinary, intentional life that is actually extraordinary because of the incredible impact and influence I have by simply following through on what I have said I will do. Yet our culture celebrates the celebrity myth, which tells us we should be famous and strive to be known simply for being well-known.

> "You can't build a reputation on what you're going to do" (Chinese philosopher Confucius).

Are we in control? Do we really have choices? The myth that we accept far too often is that we don't, but we have more control over our own lives than we often realize. I run into people all the time who say, "Man, I'm so frustrated with work, my boss, my co-workers, my spouse, my child, and I just don't know what to do. I don't really have a choice. I have to work here. I have to be married to him or her. I'm stuck in this particular situation."

But the truth is that we do have a choice. We always have a choice. We may not like the alternative of being unemployed by choosing to leave a job. We may not like having an uncomfortable conversation with our spouse. We may not like having an intense conversation with our boss or co-worker, but the truth is that we always have a choice.

We can always go out and get a different job. It might be really difficult in industries that have been hit hard by lay-offs or where a specific job is being replaced by technology. But I promise you that you always, and I rarely say always, have a choice. So take that to heart and think about that when you next hear yourself saying, "I don't have a choice."

Don't just throw your hands up in the air and say, "I don't know what to do because I'm stuck in this dead-end job, or I'm stuck in this loveless relationship, or I'm struggling with a co-worker relationship that I just can't seem to figure out." Before you throw up the white flag of surrender, think about it. You have a choice. You may not like the alternative, but you do have a choice.

"Set up your daily schedule so that it doesn't set you up."

If we don't facilitate exert planning, our days will carry us away like tidal waves, and we will feel as though things are always out of control. So schedule your day with important objectives. We all waste too much time on stuff that might be fun but won't have a long-lasting or global impact. Slowly wean yourself away from activities that are holding you back from whatever you know you need to do but aren't doing because you 'don't have time'.

Then find a system to follow up, follow up, and follow up on those objectives. Follow them through to completion and be careful not to add too many objectives at once. Get some quick, easy wins early on. Accomplish smaller, simpler tasks, then move on to others. This will get you rolling, and will psychologically carry you over the hump of excuses as to why you haven't accomplished these things before. I am always amazed at how people make half-hearted first attempts at something and then never make any further attempts. Many things we desire are within our reach if only we were a bit more persistent about follow-up and follow-through.

"Somehow over the years people have gotten the impression that Wal-Mart was...just this

> great idea that turned into an overnight success. But...it was an outgrowth of everything we'd been doing since [1945]. And like most overnight successes, it was about twenty years in the making" (Wal-Mart founder Sam Walton, quote taken from *Good to Great* by Jim Collins).

Have you ever wondered why a certain team and its leader seem to function effortlessly? Those leaders may even tell you they have a great team because they downplay their own individual efforts for the benefit of the team. But don't be deceived by this common myth; that leader has put in a lot of effort and crafted his or her leadership over time, to a point where it is possible to lead successfully. This may appear effortless because the team is such a cohesive unit. The successful leader looks for ways to continue to be efficient and effective in his or her role, thus layering skills on top of skills over time.

"You mean, non-profits work hard too?" Many fall prey to the myth that non-profits have things easier, but they don't. They just have a different set of challenges. One of those is raising money. If you work or volunteer for a non-profit and represent the organization in your community, make sure that you always have something to offer in return, rather than simply looking for handouts. It should be a win-win situation, but most non-profits make the mistake of unknowingly being perceived as greedy. If you have something to give back in exchange for what you are requesting, business people will respond positively as this rarely happens.

Too often as volunteers or employees of non-profits and churches we have a posture of 'you owe me' and 'gimme, gimme, gimme'. The mentality is that, simply because I have mentioned that I represent a non-profit or charity, your business should want to give me donations. This can take various forms, whether you are soliciting cash donations or in-kind donations.

One of the things I did to raise money for my children's private school was to talk to or email local business owners or managers. I would specifically tell them when and how often I had recently visited their restaurant, store, hotel, or other place of business. I showed them I was a regular customer and then asked for the donation, which is a much more powerful 'ask'. More often than not, I found that taking this approach increased either the chances of getting a donation or increased the donation amount. They actually paid attention to the request a bit more and considered it more thoughtfully instead of just ignoring the request as they would with other unmemorable requests.

We should remember that most of the businesspeople we're soliciting are very busy. They have a lot of responsibility, a long list of things to accomplish, and many, many charities asking them for donations, so we really have to find a way to set ourselves apart. One of the ways we can do this is by treating it as a two-way street and not, "You should donate to me because I'm a charity." The latter just isn't a good value proposition. This way, business people will be pleasantly surprised and are more likely to resonate with your strong value proposition, especially as it comes from a non-profit.

Don't always expect to be the one doing the taking. Look for the win-win and ask yourself what's in it for both parties. The expectation many non-profits and churches have that they should pay little or nothing for other organizations' products and resources (intellectual property) because they are doing ministerial or charitable work is not only wrong, but selfish and short-sighted. Many such organizations are looking for a cheaper way. Well, you get what you pay for. They will pirate software, fail to pay royalties on music and video usage, or rip off a logo or trademark without permission and still complain that they aren't growing.

Maybe if we put as much effort into strategizing what we need to do differently in order to grow and touch more lives as we did into being cheap, we might be able to move the growth needle. This is one of my pet peeves. It is so sad that people think they can skirt intellectual property rights just because they represent a charity.

Some people think working at a non-profit is easier to slack off at than in business, since non-profits don't have to work as hard. The reality is that it's just as hard, if not harder, to work for a non-profit than a for-profit business. Some people think they want to work for a non-profit, charity or ministry as the work will be fun, since they will be making a difference in others' lives. The mistake is in thinking that we'll automatically get along more easily with our co-workers and that everything will be fun. I don't think we necessarily think this consciously so much as subconsciously.

Securing volunteers is critical to serving a charitable cause. In order to be more effective in securing volunteers, ask them individually rather than collectively. A personalized, individualized request from someone they know and trust will be much more effective than a mass email or sign-up sheet, but many people still use these tools. The reality is that people don't respond to that sort of call to action as they would do if it was personalized to them and their knowledge, skills, and experience.

If you ask collectively it is unlikely that you will get many committed volunteers. I have seen this time and time again, but even when I explain it, most people look at me as though I have two heads and choose not to modify their method of asking. Later, they end up complaining again that they can't get enough volunteers.

If you go to Susie and say, "I know you do XYZ well and think you would be a really great fit for this singular volunteering opportunity", Susie will most likely say yes. We don't need more volunteers; we just need better methods of personally engaging them in a way that draws them to the opportunity. So strive to make that personal ask and I promise you'll achieve much better results.

23

Manage My Boss? Seize Responsibility and Autonomy?

What? I need to manage my boss? Shouldn't it be my boss' responsibility to manage me? Well, that's only half true. Managing a business relationship effectively is a two-way street. Now, you don't *have* to manage up the chain of command, but you will be less effective in your current role and your long-term career if you don't.

Also, beware when a new boss steps in. He or she probably has a different management style, pet peeves, and preferences compared with your previous boss. Don't assume that what worked before will work now. When you acquire a new boss, be sure to change your style to match his or hers rather than expecting the new manager to change to yours. "Elementary, my dear Miles," you say, and you're right. It should be common sense.

So much of our work life is about getting into a rhythm or flow with our coworkers, direct reports, and bosses. Some people would rather not find a way to work together as a team; they want to be lone wolves. We all have idiosyncrasies; it's just a matter of how we can work together given that fact. Often we want our bosses or peers to change to fit our style when we really have to be the ones to adapt. If we don't, the outcome usually isn't good. You may be demoted or moved to another department, or in some extreme cases actually lose your job.

While we never want to mislead anyone, it is important to manage our bosses' and peers' perceptions of us. Rarely commit a project or deadline to your superior without talking and seeking feedback or input from a peer or the subordinate who will have to do the work. Skipping the feedback step sets both you and your boss up for failure, in that you may overcommit to something that the person beneath you can't deliver, either on time or at all.

It might seem tempting to delay your boss' pet project, but if you complete his or her projects first your manager won't be on your back, continually asking why a certain project still hasn't been completed. Even if you don't think it's incredibly important, refrain from debating over the merits. If you agree to do it, get it done. This will increase your credibility and free you up to do the other stuff that you perceive to be more important.

Likewise, the perception of how hard we work is important. Perhaps you should send a few emails outside of normal business hours. Or you may want to wait to turn in a project for a day or two after you have completed it, unless you have a deadline. That doesn't mean you should coast while you're waiting to turn in work; it is likely that you have other projects to work on that are in various stages of completion. You simply don't want to give the impression that you can crank out work too fast or you may find yourself deluged.

Speaking poorly about your boss behind his or her back, even in confidence to your peers, is never a good idea. It's okay to express frustration behind closed doors, but be careful when you do this because even though you may think it is done in secret, your boss may have a way of finding out that information. An alternative is to find a respectful way to communicate to your boss that he or she is causing frustration in a particular area. Not all leaders will be open to this, mind you, but being able to professionally and graciously express frustration to a superior without fearing their wrath is a sign of a healthy boss-staff relationship. Anything other than that is simply unhealthy.

Why is it that our bosses always seem to think they have an answer and a solution to our problems? We wind up thinking, "Why didn't I think of that? I should be able to think of that kind of solution." I've wrestled with this frustration myself. My boss might think that I can't come up with solutions on my own, but I've been on both sides of the fence and know that sometimes the boss is in a different frame of mind and isn't as close to the situation, which allows him or her to think more clearly, or more strategically, or at a higher level. This doesn't mean that the boss always has an easier time coming up with a solution; it's just that having a different perspective allows him or her space to think more creatively, so just be comfortable with this and understand the dynamic of being on either side of that fence.

Don't try to curry favor with your boss' boss because this will likely anger your manager and put him or her in a bad position. You should be interested in making your boss look good and then it's his or her job to make his or her own manager look good. Don't try to jump that extra layer of leadership. This will naturally happen as a by-product of helping your boss look good if they see the valuable work you're doing. Trying to go around your boss can cause all kinds of political problems and ultimately it's just not your responsibility.

Allow your manager to take the projects you have worked on to his or her boss rather than showing them off yourself. Sometimes the only way your boss will give up decision-making control is to take more responsibility and autonomy away from him or her. This isn't to be taken lightly, and you should skillfully and diplomatically manage this, but sometimes it's the only way to gain more latitude, autonomy, and the ability to work within a broader scope.

The key to getting your boss to stop telling you how to do your job is to get results. It is hard to argue with results, although extreme micromanagers will still find a way. If your performance is strong and is beating your boss' expectations, it is very unlikely that he or she will continue to tell you how to do your job. If they do, they're foolish, and you probably shouldn't be working for them anyhow.

24

Digital Marketing Mashup

Marketing and sales functions are interdependent if they work well together, but are two completely different animals. However, many people talk about sales and marketing in the same breath as if they serve the same function. Marketing teams draw in leads, and sales teams typically close the deal. Now, sales may share some of the responsibility in soliciting leads with their salespeople's 'boots on the ground', but generally this is where the lines are drawn between sales and marketing.

The challenge comes when the sales department blames marketing for failing to provide enough leads or for providing too many poor-quality leads. Then marketing lobs a grenade over the wall and says that the salespeople need to close more of the valued leads the marketing department is working so hard to gain.

What I've just described is a dysfunctional marketing and sales relationship, if you can even call it a relationship. A more healthy alliance depicts both teams as partners in developing solutions together. Blame, for the most part, doesn't exist. Both teams methodically work together to achieve better-quality leads and to turn them into sales. Don't make the mistake of thinking that marketing and sales are the same thing; they aren't.

When communicating a marketing project that needs to be carried out, be it graphic design, video, or website, the more planning, preparation, and specific examples of other similar concepts and ideas you can give to those involved, the better, less expensive, and quicker the finished product will be. Many people make the mistake of saying, "I don't know what I want, so I have no ideas. Just go do it." But the more you can mock up, sketch out, storyboard, wireframe, or pencil out the copy, look and feel, colors, and layout the better.

You may think that you are doing the graphic designers' or website designers' or videographers' jobs for them. To some extent that is true, but the more input you give, the more likely that the output will be closer to your vision and the less time it will take to go back and forth and revise it five or six times, since it wasn't clearly communicated at the beginning. Maybe you don't think you know what you want. Please take the time; slow down. Discipline yourself to think it through, and you'll be much more likely to have your vision realized, and in a shorter amount of time.

"It is either an exciting or scary time to be a marketer."

Those who spend the most to acquire a customer always win. While this may seem counterintuitive as we always want to minimize our marketing expenses, our competitors won't be able to compete if we spend more than them in acquiring our customers. We will own the market. And if we consider and maximize the lifetime customer value, an organization can afford to pay more to acquire that customer in the first place.

Larger organizations will grow stronger than smaller organizations, which will get smaller and weaker due to

134

the challenging economy and the fact that online marketing is becoming much more technical, sophisticated, and costly, unless we can find a way to use that size and advantage against them. Either way, it will still cost a pretty penny.

Gone are the Wild West days of cheap and easy SEO work. Ten years ago, it was a gold rush; people were basically printing money online. This income inequality will affect organizations just as it is affecting the income prospects of many. There are no magic bullets in marketing or in business in general, so don't fall for that fallacy. While we should quantify the returns on our marketing expenditures whenever possible, it is very tricky to do so.

We need to balance direct marketing (with a clear return on investment and short-term goals) and branding efforts, which are a long-term play. It would seem as though it is easy to track all online marketing efforts due to technological advances. It is certainly easier than it used to be, just not as simple as we might think.

There are tools such as call tracking and form submission tracking that indicate which online campaign has prompted a purchase and which campaign was responsible for that final action, but it cannot indicate all the other marketing campaigns a customer may have seen before they took that final action. And we have to assume that each of those marketing campaigns earned part of the sales conversion attribution.

We might think that campaign A isn't working, since it isn't converting sales quantifiably, while campaign B is hitting it out of the park. But campaign A might be the main way people hear about your product or service, while campaign B just happens to be the closing channel. This highlights how misleading tracking can be.

25

Ignore Money and Board Issues
at Your Own Peril

At times, we must carefully exclude certain sunk costs from consideration during a business decision. Unintentionally, we often include past money spent on future decisions. We may shy away from killing a pet project, but we shouldn't continue to throw good money after bad. We should disassociate ourselves from money spent in the past in order to make a logical decision to continue viable projects into the future.

A number of years ago, I purchased a number of domain names for various future business ventures I had envisioned at the time. I bought a few here and a few there, and, over time, it got to the point where I was paying hundreds of dollars each month in annual domain renewal fees. So I decided to cut a few domains, but since I was emotionally invested in the money I had spent renewing certain domains for the previous six years, that was a difficult decision to make. Eventually, I ruthlessly pared back the number of domains by ninety percent, keeping only the ones I had specific plans to use. Had I done this sooner, I would have saved even more money. Remember that a sunk cost isn't worth considering when deciding whether to continue or kill a project.

Not only is the way we view and manage true business expenses important; how others view the way we separate personal and business issues is also significant. Should we have our assistants take on personal tasks for us to free us up to work on more productive tasks? I know many business owners who would respond to this question with a resounding "Yes!" And while I won't disagree that they can do whatever they want if they are the primary owner or CEO/president, we need to be thoughtful about how others will perceive an assistant regularly picking up our dry cleaning or paying our personal bills.

Another area of caution is the line between personal and business expenses, especially as you rise further up the leadership ladder. As we do so, we have more control over larger budgets and are afforded certain liberties to purchase additional items for our own professional benefit. Don't be afraid to use business funds for your own or other team members' professional development. You may even want to take your team out to lunch as a reward. Just don't abuse this freedom and make sure that there isn't even any appearance of abuse.

It may become easier to justify something that was once a personal expense as a business one. For example, perhaps you are at a networking lunch that could genuinely benefit you and/or your company. Do you pull out your company credit card to pay or your own? You can see the dilemma, right? Sometimes things are grey instead of black and white. Now, the credit card charge may be legitimate, but we should take a minute to pause and genuinely reflect on that decision rather than making it hastily.

If you use your business card for obvious personal expenses, you could get yourself in trouble with the IRS if you try to deduct them as legitimate business expenses. Even if you don't deduct them from your taxes, it just doesn't look good to your employees. If you think you're hiding it, you are only fooling yourself. Someone in your organization, at the very least someone from accounting, has seen it. So why lose credibility over an issue like this? It isn't worth it.

Wages are usually one of the top business expense items, so this is an important money issue for leaders to wade through. Discussion among staff about how much each person makes is a hot topic, for sure. Whether we believe that everyone should know everyone else's pay level or that no one but HR and the direct supervisor should know, it's still unprofessional to discuss our salary levels with co-workers and inappropriate to discuss how much we make with our direct reports.

While I believe that sales and marketing people should be more highly compensated than anyone else in the organization, assuming they are exceeding their goals, I am generally against incentive pay due to the conflict of interest inherent in unethical people 'gaming' the incentive pay system. Sadly, this almost always happens to some degree. So be very cautious if you are planning to implement a performance-based incentive and make sure you try to anticipate unintended consequences.

I lean more towards paying team members a generous base pay and supplementing this minimally on performance. This doesn't mean we shouldn't monitor employee performance; far from it. If employees are performing consistently well, increase their base pay. Don't tempt them to think too much about bonus pay. Too much incentive-based pay tends to focus people's attention on working the system to gain as much bonus pay as possible, even if you have ethical team members. Employees may not be as focused on what benefits the customer and company first if bonuses are in play. If performance-based pay is important to you, it is even more important to hire morally focused team members who will do the right thing for the customer and organization, regardless of the pay system.

When budgeting, start with a top-down approach, then bottom-up. Top-down starts with what revenue is needed to cover projected expenses, and bottom-up seeks to minimize expenses to determine the least amount of revenue needed to cover them. This makes you think at a high level first; then you will see how accurate your rough top-down version was when doing a more detailed, bottom-up calculation.

When forced to make budget cuts, cut fat not bone. The amount of fat you have in your organization will determine how deeply you need to cut before you get to the bone. Every organization is different. Some need to cut deeper and some need to cut in a more shallow way. The tendency is almost always to cut in too shallow a way. We need to find a balance between the two, where our cuts don't cripple the team but are substantial enough to avoid making further cuts a couple of months down the line. Cuts have the added benefit of shaking things up, giving the potential for growth and new life. But given the choice, I would err on the side of making cuts that are slightly too deep rather than too shallow.

Broader macroeconomic issues can and often do affect businesses and non-profits, yet most organizations are unaware of these economic indicators. Economists have defined some as 'leading' economic indicators and others as 'lagging'. Leading indicators can be used, to some extent, to predict economic booms or busts, while lagging indicators are only used to see things in the rear-view mirror.

If we confuse the two, we can make poor decisions as leaders. For example, if we look at recent charitable giving to find out how the economy is doing as a leading indicator, this would be flawed, since that indicator is lagging.

Leading economic indicators include the stock market, retail sales, and the housing market. However, be careful when it comes to leading indicators. They could also be misleading as they depend on the sentiment of the population. Lagging indicators include GDP, unemployment, inflation, interest rates, and corporate profits, so make sure you know the difference. The government may lead us to either believe that inflation is a sign of growth or a sign of economic contraction, and to some extent both have merit.

But this glosses over the finer details. Deflationary environments penalize savers. And inflationary (including hyperinflationary) environments tear at the very fabric of our society because it undermines trust in currency and the ability to buy, sell, and trade using that currency. When that trust is broken and it reaches critical mass, normally functioning markets are distorted and it changes the way people do business and conduct their own personal finances.

Another danger area to watch out for involves the board of directors. Don't add someone to your board just because they're a high-net-worth individual. Add them because they're going to add value in some way that you currently lack. It makes no sense to add a fundraiser when your organization is in desperate need of a finance professional to help spearhead your first audit.

The reasons board members are asked to join will change over time, so you may need to help a board member leave the organization. Often those who are self-aware know when their time is up, while others who are less aware tend to stay when the need they once filled is no longer there.

As tempting as it is reach out to board members that you don't immediately report to, it is only a matter of time before this will cause gossip and other complications (seemingly contradicting something your boss, who reports directly to the board, has stated to the board him or herself). Even though it is tempting to directly show these people your work and how well you've done, that communication is likely to get back to your boss or to HR, so you should tread very cautiously in that area.

Another couple of challenging areas involving boards include gossip based on partial or complete misinformation, and failing to respect the executive chain of command and authority. In order to minimize these issues, boards should seriously consider opting for a Policy Governance model to clearly define appropriate and inappropriate channels of communication and boundaries for everyone who is involved with board members.

I was part of a non-profit that implemented this specific standard, and it cleared up much of the confusion over what the board and executive team should do versus what they shouldn't do. Role clarity for boards is vital to a healthy, functioning executive team and organization.

If you report directly to the board, communication is key to a successful executive tenure. Keeping them apprised of issues ahead of an upcoming board meeting will help you to avoid blindsiding them with information they aren't prepared to discuss. You would be surprised at how many leaders don't do this with their boards. They just come to the board meeting with all their great ideas or overwhelm them with every little detail of the organization.

You don't want to tempt them to micromanage you by giving them too many details, but you don't want to go to the other extreme either, where they have little idea of what's going on. So don't be afraid to give information to the board ahead of time so its members can prepare. You may think it could be used against you, but usually it is quite the opposite if you have a well-functioning board. This will breed trust and understanding so that the board is prepared for your presentation and requests. You are more likely to get things passed if they have a few days or weeks to prepare.

26

Closing Thoughts:
Don't Be a NAG

"I've learned that making a 'living' is not the
same thing as 'making a life' (Maya Angelou,
taken from her poem, *I've Learned*).

Don't be a narcissistic, arrogant guy/gal (NAG). Nobody
likes a nag. And if we're honest with ourselves, we are
profoundly guilty of this in our culture today. We think
that self-happiness is the goal, but joy comes from serving others: our bosses, peers, co-workers, direct reports,
board members, family and friends. In fact, you don't
even have to be happy to have joy. Selfless service is
filled with joy and reward that outweighs what we give
up in sacrifice. Choose your path wisely. By choosing
servant leadership you won't ever be disappointed on
your deathbed. To borrow a phrase from Men's Wear-
house founder, George Zimmer, "I guarantee it!"

To thank you for purchasing the paperback or ebook
version of *Why Leadership Sucks Volume Two*, I am
giving you my audiobook on a completely complimentary basis! Whoa, wait a cotton-pickin' minute! "Did I
hear you right, Miles?" Yes, you did. All I ask in exchange
is that you provide your email address... the one you
regularly use (not your generic signup email addy). Hey,
I spend a ton of my own time and money recording,
editing, mastering, and publishing my audiobook on

Audible, iTunes, and Amazon, so it's only fair for you to supply me with a real email address, and I'm happy to provide you with the complimentary audiobook in exchange. And it's not an abridged version; it's the entire audiobook.

To get it, go to

milesanthonysmith.com/wls2audiobook

and use password GIMMEMYWLS2AUDIOBOOK. Go check it out right now. You can listen again while driving, working out, cooking or doing a range of other activities.

My Current and Forthcoming Books and Resources

Why Leadership Sucks Volume One:
Fundamentals of Level 5 Leadership and
Servant Leadership

Currently available online in ebook, paperback, and audio book formats

> "It is literally true that you can succeed best and quickest by *helping* others to succeed."
>
> (Author Napoleon Hill)

What is leadership? How do we define leadership? What is servant leadership? What are the most effective leadership characteristics? Do you wish your company had a leadership development program, or are you frustrated with organizational leadership? Do you wonder why some leadership styles suck? You are not alone.

So why does leadership suck? It sucks because real leadership is hard, requires selfless service, and because the buck stops with you. Servant leadership or Level 5 leadership is uncomfortable, humbling, self-denying, painful, and counterintuitive. Nonetheless, it is the only kind of leadership that brings lasting results, genuine happiness, and true self-fulfillment.

If you haven't read volume one of the *Why Leadership Sucks* series, be sure to pick it up!

Why Leadership Sucks Online Video Course

Currently available at Udemy.com

Miles and Christopher Paul Elliott will guide your leadership journey to increase leadership IQ and enhance effectiveness using real-world examples. Chris is a servant leadership speaker and author of *Thought Shredder*. Video sessions include: Self-Awareness, First Impressions Are Lasting Impressions... As Long As You Let Them Last, and Are you a Micromanager or a Macromanager?

If you enjoyed either volume one or two of the Why Leadership Sucks books, plug into these thirty-three lectures with a full ninety minutes of video packed with actionable insights, bonus MP3s, PowerPoints, and other resources.

Becoming Generation Flux: How to Build an Agile, Adaptable, and Resilient Career

Currently available online in ebook, paperback, and audio book formats

"The illiterate of the 21st century will not be those who cannot read or write, but those who cannot learn, unlearn, and relearn."

(Futurist Alvin Toffler)

The new currency of a successful career is to find a niche where we bring value that not many others can. No longer is a good work ethic enough to secure and retain a job with middle-class pay and benefits as it was a generation ago. My forthcoming book, *Becoming Generation Flux: How to Build an Agile, Adaptable, and Resilient Career*, will address this change in employment and how to navigate the new work environment.

The Serial Specialist: Who They Are and Why You MUST Hire Them to Thrive

"The division of labour offers us the first example of how, as long as man remains in natural society, that is as long as a cleavage exists between the particular and the common interest, as long therefore as activity is not voluntarily, but naturally, divided, man's own deed becomes an alien power opposed to him, which enslaves him instead of being controlled by him. For as soon as labour is distributed, each man has a particular, exclusive sphere of activity, which is forced upon him and from which he cannot escape."

(Socialist Karl Marx)

"Specialization may be all well very well if you happen to have skills particularly suited to these jobs, or if you are passionate about a niche area of work, and of course there is also the benefit of feeling pride in being considered an expert. But there is equally the danger of becoming dissatisfied by the repetition inherent in many specialist professions...

"Moreover, our culture of specialization conflicts with something most of us intuitively recognize, but which career advisers are only beginning to understand: we each have multiple selves... We have complex, multi-faceted experiences, interests, values and talents, which might mean that we could also find fulfillment as a web designer, or a community police officer, or running an organic cafe.

"This is a potentially liberating idea with radical implications. It raises the possibility that we might discover career fulfillment by escaping the confines of specialization and cultivating ourselves as wide achievers...allowing the various petals of our identity to fully unfold."

(Philosopher Roman Krznaric)

Do you hire specialists in your specific industry but continually feel disappointed with their innovation and creativity levels? Are you routinely rejecting generalists for fear of them not sticking around very long? Or are you frustrated with your own career, sensing a kind of indentured servitude to your particular work specialty?

Do you yearn to do other things? Do you get bored after a few years in one type of work?

If so, *The Serial Specialist* is for you. Miles will help you understand why these outliers are typically outcasts but should be brought into your corporate fold to achieve success in this challenging economy. You will learn why you and they are to be highly valued, and how to identify, hire, and retain adaptable, agile, and innovative talent.

Look out for it in 2018.

Recruiting and Retaining Generation Flux: Why Traditional Tactics Won't Hire Top Talent

> "A master in the art of living draws no sharp distinction between his work and his play; his labor and his leisure; his mind and his body; his education and his recreation. He hardly knows which is which. He simply pursues his vision of excellence through whatever he is doing, and leaves others to determine whether he is working or playing. To himself, he always appears to be doing both."
>
> (L.P. Jacks, taken from *Education through Recreation*)

Are you straining to source the right talent from a pool of new workers, those gainfully employed (and concerned about stability and security) or those in career transition? Does the candidate pool appear to contain fewer people with the right skills and character? Does your HR role feel stressful; as though you are trying to find needles in a world where the hay is more widely scattered? If so, *Recruiting and Retaining Generation Flux* is for you.

Are you struggling to stem the turnover tide of retiring boomers without having enough qualified Generation X staff or Millennials to plug those holes? Perhaps you're frustrated with traditional human resources development and retention tactics that don't seem to be as effective or successful as before.

Miles will guide you on a journey to help you understand the talent-sourcing past, confront the candidate-selection present, and conquer future retention success. You will learn why traditional recruiting and retention tactics are dead and how to identify, hire, and retain adaptable, agile, innovative, and resilient talent no matter what the market throws your way.

Look out for it in 2020.

The Opportunity Cost of Christ

"We drive our cars 60-70 miles per hour with an oncoming car doing the same with only a white line and six to eight feet separating us. We place our faith that every car will not cross into our lane. We fly on airplanes that take us over oceans, trusting the pilots with our very lives. We ride on thrilling amusement rides that take us several stories into the air and travel fifty to seventy miles per hour down a winding slope. We trust the operators of that ride with our own mortality.

"There is a great irony in the fact that we can place our faith in such things but cannot place our faith in the hands of our Creator."

(Os Hillman, taken from marketplaceleaders.org)

We all have faith and trust in many features of modern life, seeking the allusion of security. Among them are a paper money system, accumulated wealth, relationships, food, alcohol, government, business, and education. We even believe that the brakes on our cars will stop us and that doctors will heal our ailments. So why do we have such a hard time putting our faith and trust in Christ?

My forthcoming book, *The Opportunity Cost of Christ*, argues that trusting in and following Christ is not a leap of faith in defiance of reason, but the reasonable conclusion of a rational mind.

Look out for it in 2022.

Other Leadership Books I Recommend

- *Blue Ocean Strategy* by W. Chan Kim and Renée Mauborgne
- *The One Minute Manager* by Kenneth H. Blanchard
- *The 1% Windfall* by Rafi Mohammed
- *Dare to Serve* by Cheryl Bachelder
- *Leaders Eat Last* by Simon Sinek
- *The Score Takes Care of Itself* by Bill Walsh, Joe Montana, Steve Jamison, and Craig Walsh
- *The Myths of Creativity* by David Burkus
- *On Becoming a Leader* by Warren G. Bennis
- *True North* by Bill George
- *Rumsfeld's Rules* by Donald Rumsfeld
- *Lead Like Jesus* by Ken Blanchard and Phil Hodges
- *It Worked for Me* by Colin Powell
- Any of Peter Drucker's books
- Any of Robert K. Greenleaf's books
- Any of John C. Maxwell's books

About the Author

Miles Anthony Smith, an ambivert and serial specialist, has held senior, executive leadership positions for businesses and non-profits over the past fifteen years. He has broad management skills across many functional business disciplines in accounting, finance, human resources, marketing, and leadership, earning a Bachelor of Music Composition degree from Oral Roberts University and a master's in Business Administration from Oklahoma State University. Miles currently works for Mr. Rekey, America's largest residential locksmith® as director of digital marketing. Miles is the author of the *Why Leadership Sucks* and the *Generation Flux* series.

Born a Hoosier, raised an Okie, and currently residing in the frozen tundra of Green Bay, Wisconsin, Miles is happily married to Carolyn and is a proud father of three. Now in his mid-thirties, he was fortunate to have been given a significant leadership opportunity by his father at the age of twenty-five. He is a classically trained violist, violinist, and composer, with passions in the fields of small-business management, marketing, macroeconomics, servant leadership, and classical education.

Miles, a Generation X leader and author, cares enough about organizational health to make the tough decisions, hire and coach the right people, set clear expectations, develop a strong team culture, and strengthen organizational cash flow, exhibiting both humility and fierce resolve. His mission in life is: "To chart the course, pave the pathway, and light the lane for others to eclipse my own success in leadership."